LIFESTYLE
STORES

Martin M. Pegler

Architecture & Interior Design Library

AN IMPRINT OF
PBC INTERNATIONAL, INC.

Distributor to the book trade in the United States and Canada
Rizzoli International Publications
through St. Martin's Press
175 Fifth Avenue
New York, NY 10010

Distributor to the art trade in the United States and Canada
PBC International, Inc.
One School Street
Glen Cove, NY 11542

Distributor throughout the rest of the world
Hearst Books International
1350 Avenue of the Americas
New York, NY 10019

Library of Congress Cataloging–in–Publication Data

Pegler, Martin M.
Lifestyle stores / by Martin Pegler
        p.   cm.
    Includes index.
    ISBN 0-86636-498-6 (alk. paper). — ISBN 0-86636-499-4 (pbk.alk. paper).
    1. Stores, Retail.—Social aspects. 2. Display of merchandise—Pyschological aspects.
    3. Stores, Retail.—Design and construction. 4. Lifestyle—Economic aspects. 5. Sales promotion. I. Title
HF5429.P395 1996   96–15789
381'.1—dc20   CIP

CAVEAT– Information in this text is believed accurate, and will pose no
problem for the student or casual reader. However, the author was often
constrained by information contained in signed release forms, information
that could have been in error or not included at all. Any misinformation
(or lack of information) is the result of failure in these attestations. The
author has done whatever is possible to insure accuracy.

Designed by Garrett Schuh

Color separation by Fine Arts Repro House Co. Ltd., Hong Kong
Printing and binding by Dai Nippon Printing Group

10 9 8 7 6 5 4 3 2 1

Printed in Hong Kong

To Larry—without whom this book would not have happened.

Contents

Foreword

"The customer will never notice the details." That's a comment everyone in the retail industry has heard more than once. You're tucked away in some creative room, three hours into a one-hour meeting, and your energy is flagging. You've worked and reworked a shop concept a dozen times and it still looks exactly as it did when you started. Suddenly, in the middle of yet another debate about balance, focus, and point of view, somebody throws up his hands and says, "C'mon, people—the customer's never gonna notice any of these details!"

GAP For shame. What arrogance. What presumptuousness. What ignorance. The customer is going to notice. The customer always notices. And to dismiss the customer as uninterested, imperceptive, or—worst of all—unworthy, is to dismiss the very reason we do what we do.

The fact is, the retail industry exists for the customer. Those of us working in retail design should understand this better than anyone. The customer is our maker and judge. We live or die every time one walks into—or by—one of our stores.

And make no mistake, there's a lot of "walking by" going on today. Retail design has become incredibly competitive. No longer will the customer look beyond a shoebox storefront—even if the goods inside are gold. No longer will the customer navigate a rough sea of racks and rounders and awkwardly dressed mannequins—even if the fashion on display is right on. No longer will the customer tolerate long lines and indifferent service—even if the prices are dynamite. The customer has come to expect more—more creativity, more comfort, more excitement, more value. In short, more detail.

In this book you will see that great store design exists in the details. It's in this light fixture and that flooring treatment. It's this twist and that turn. And while all these little details may not seem significant by themselves, taken together—and assembled in the right place for the right reason—they create a environment that not only attracts customers, it captures and keeps them.

And (lest we forget) that's what it's all about.

~ MARK DVORAK, Vice President, Visual Design, *Gap, Inc.*

The days of the quiet, orderly little general store are gone. Merchandising has become entertainment: spinning signs, flashing lights, thumping music. We've got video screens, interactive computer kiosks, playhouses and day care for the kids. Some of us even offer in-store cafes, with soup and sandwiches for hungry shoppers.

It's all part of the retail industry's effort to win consumers' leisure time—a limited commodity these days, to be sure. Between work and family and school and fitness, there's not a lot of time left for a trip to the mall. As a result, we retailers feel we'd better make it good or else our customers may opt for a movie, or a ballgame, or an excursion on the Internet.

Throughout the industry—and throughout this book—there are signs of unprecedented merchandising creativity. And we're not talking about color-coded stacks of T-shirts, either. The approaches illustrated here, while widely varied, demonstrate that time-tested merchandising concepts such as focus, impact, and coordination can and do coexist with more contemporary, entertainment-oriented elements like movement, change, surprise, and humor.

A cautionary note, however: This new wave of "retail entertainment" brings with it some real dangers. After all, entertainment for its own sake has no value. As retailers, we must continually ask ourselves: Are we losing sight of the products we're selling? Are we forgetting the "merchandise" in "merchandising"?

Effective visual merchandising has a purpose. It creates awareness of brands and products. It communicates freshness and excitement and change in a store. It enhances the goods and boosts sales.

In some cases, visual merchandising even inspires product design. And that's when you know it's really working. Because when our products and store environments become truly interdependent, we create a synergy—a "lifestyle," if you will—that actually consumes the consumer.

Now that's entertainment.

~ **JODY PATRAKA**, Vice President, Visual Merchandising, *Old Navy Clothing Co.*

Introduction

"Lifestyle" is the current buzzword in retailing. We hear it applied to the clothes we wear, the furniture and furnishings we use to fill our homes, the cars we drive, and the magazines we read. Lifestyle refers to the way we live—the things we do—the places we go and where we eat. With our preferences we create a way of life, an attitude and an image of what we are or what we hope to be perceived as being—similar to going to a costume ball where you dress as the person you would like to be.

Lifestyle shopping is an egocentric experience, because you shop for the inner self—the real you. You may only spend two weeks a year on a golfing vacation, but your lifestyle may be a year-round investment in selecting the clothes, the clubs, the monogrammed tees, the paraphernalia that identify you as a golfer for the other fifty weeks. Selecting an auto can be a lifestyle decision: do you pick something racy, daring and wild—or should the car be more in keeping with your professional status? Where you eat and what you eat can also be lifestyle directed. Faddish foods? Exotic foods? Healthy foods? If you have always longed for a life of travel and adventure, each "foreign" dining experience can be part of your "wanderlust" style. Every safari-inspired garment you buy puts your dream into virtual reality. When we shop lifestyle, we find the time to shop and savor the shopping experience, because we are shopping for something that really counts in our lives.

The "weekend handyman"—the time-frustrated builder/architect/designer/carpenter—savors being let loose in a 100,000-square-foot mega-store filled with tools, timber, building materials, fittings and finishes and much more. This is paradise! This is his/her world. Book lovers can also spend hours thumbing through books or just breathing in the smell of the printed page; if they can do it over a cup of coffee then time stands still and the world stops spinning. The fit and fitness enthusiast can spend more time selecting the

proper pair of athletic shoes than in buying a pair of shoes for a date. He or she may have a wardrobe of sport shoes, each for a specialized sports use.

For some, the very act of shopping has become a lifestyle. More and more shoppers are looking for value, in-depth selection, comfort, convenience and economy of time. With free time a priority, the shopping expedition has also become a family adventure, especially where the family shares a lifestyle. Many lifestyle retailers—like those in this book—have operations that attract, amuse and entertain the entire family. The giant book stores have an area where kids can play or read while the parents browse their own interests. The sporting goods stores have specific scaled-down, "touch-try-play" areas set aside for the younger family members while adults can shoot, throw, putt or aim in the grown-up playgrounds. Many mega-stores now have food courts or coffee/soft drink bars integrated into the store design to protract the family visit and make it even more enjoyable.

The book has been divided into five major lifestyle categories that include how we dress—how and where we live—and some of the things we like to do when we have the time to do them. There are many more lifestyles but we have attempted to compress as many as we could into the five chapters.

Have a *HAPPY* lifestyle.

~ MARTIN M. PEGLER

Home Improvement

The **1990s** may eventually become known to future generations as "the era of cocooning." Indeed, as people are spending increasingly more time at home, home entertainment centers and offices have turned the concept of home into far more than the place where the heart and hearth are—it is the **center** of everything.

Homemakers come in all shapes and sizes in the 1990s. They can be weekend do-it-yourselfers, groundskeepers, gardeners, furniture

refinishers, or wallpaper hangers. Their true lifestyle calling might simply be classified as "home improvement," but they often **design**, **construct, and decorate** with another lifestyle in mind. Some are modernists, some are traditionalists; some would like to have lived in the French provinces during the reign of Louis XV, while others think of home as a hunting lodge in the woods. The clutter of collections in an early-

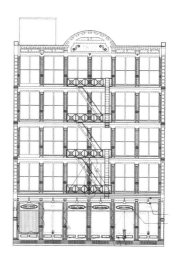

American home appeals to some; others prefer the chaste, clean lines of Milanese modern.

Furniture and home furnishings stores frequently display merchandise on "pods" or stages where a particular period, style, or  lifestyle is represented, complete with all of the appropriate acces- sories and accouterments. Some shoppers are so focused  on a **specific lifestyle** that they may shop exclusively in specialty shops such as Eddie Bauer or Out of the West (see "The Living is Easy"). The greatest number of "homers," however, find their ***solutions*** in the mega supply stores like those included in this chapter, where fashion is introduced in tandem with decorating advice and technical guidance. Home can be your **castle,** cottage, or cabin; it all depends upon your lifestyle.

Pottery Barn

A division of Williams-Sonoma, Inc., Pottery Barn is noted for its three primary product lines: tabletop, decorative accessories, and home furnishings. Pottery Barn stores have appeared in many upscale malls, but to enhance presentation and market their full range of products as shown in the catalog, the company is currently establishing flagship stores in major cities around the country.

The basic concept for the design of these freestanding outlets involves the adaptive reuse of urban lofts and loft-type buildings. This 6,658-square-foot store on Chestnut Street in San Francisco juxtaposes old against new, and its facade recalls the classicism of the Panama Pacific Exhibition that was held on the same site in 1914.

Inside, the airy, two-story-high space is crowned with a pyramid-shaped skylight that floods the neutral interior with sunlight. The walls are either exposed raw concrete left over from the original structure, or warm-hued Italian plaster. Natural cedar boards and exposed wood joists adorn the ceiling. The rear of the space has been converted into a "design studio," where the home furnishings collections are displayed. Intended to provide a single location for customers to assemble various elements and materials for furnishing their homes, the hub of the design studio is a massive, six-foot by twelve-foot wooden table, where fabrics, plans, and accessories can be laid out and reviewed side by side. Staff is available to assist customers in making selections and to answer questions about any of the materials in the design studio.

By employing fundamental materials like concrete, Venetian marble, yellow pine, and red cedar, "everything feels homey and natural," says Gary Friedman, executive vice president of Williams-Sonoma. The design is an ageless synthesis of classical and modern elements in which the merchandise can be artfully and prominently displayed.

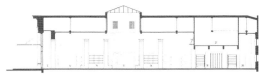

Designer/Architect: Backen Arrigoni & Ross, Inc.
Principal-in-charge: Howard Backen
Project Managers: Hans Baldauf, Ken Jung
Project Architects: Chris Cahill, Tim Chappelle, Jim Ritter, Gary Schilling, Charles Theobald, Tim Wong

For Williams-Sonoma, Inc., San Francisco
Architectural Consultant: Richard Altuna
Director of Store Development: Foster Cope III
Director of Visual Merchandising: Parry Yohannan
Design Coordinator: Patti Kashima
In-Store Visuals: Mauricio Arias

Photography: Douglas Dun

San Francisco, California

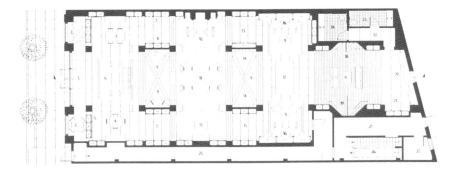

15

DESIGN STUDIO

DESIGN STUDIO

"Everything

feels homey and natural..."

Smith & Hawken

From the weekend or full-time gardener to the fire escape, rooftop, or greenhouse horticulturist to anyone with a desire to green one's thumb, Smith & Hawken caters to the whims and wants of a variety of back-to-nature devotees.

Located in an 1872 landmark building in New York's SoHo, this Smith & Hawken store was designed to adapt itself to the existing structure and space. In this instance, the entrance doors were chosen specifically because they were in keeping with the tradition of the existing facade, although the spade and fork garden tools do make unique and contrasting handle fixtures. The interior is warm and welcoming. Exposed brick walls and natural, often reclaimed, wood is used on the floor and as shelving to reinforce the desired, timeless look. The designers' objective was to create the feeling of a small-town business, where comfortable conversation between customers and staff can take place in a relaxed, unhurried atmosphere.

Hutch-like shelving fixtures line the exposed brick and concrete walls and display an assortment of terra-cotta and ceramic pots, tools, and other products geared toward the urban gardener. The exposed galvanized heating ducts and raw materials and textures all add to "the potting shed aesthetic," which is both unexpected and refreshing in a city store. The hub of this warm and woodsy space is a semicircular cash/wrap desk garnished with house plants and topiaries. Long rows of track lighting illuminate the space, while several low-voltage lamps add lively accents of brightness and color to an otherwise neutral setting.

Architect/Designer: **Hill/Glazier Architects, Inc.**
Principal-in-charge: **Robert Glazier**
Contractor: **Richter & Ratner**
Photography: **Chun Y Lai**

New York, **New York**

IKEA Marketing Outpost

Shoppers who enjoy finding new and different items to accent their homes and lifestyles will find the perfect resource in the new IKEA Marketing Outpost in midtown Manhattan. Rather than the freestanding mega-stores that IKEA usually plants along major highways, this 7,500-square-foot, two-level space, tucked inside a multi-story building, presents samplings of various IKEA product lines. Bus service shuttles interested customers from this display center to the comprehensive IKEA warehouse in nearby Elizabeth, New Jersey.

To enhance the adaptable "stage set" concept for this outpost, the architects and designers of Walker Group/CNI devised totally modular wall units which correspond to an eight-foot grid system located in the ceiling and floor. The two-foot by four-foot maple timber and metal grids suspended from the ceiling are complemented by the wooden grids in the natural concrete floor. Maple panels, supporting up to 150 pounds each, can be hung from the suspended grid and then anchored to the floor. In addition, lightweight graphics panels of various colors can be worked into the grid configuration; by rearranging the panels, new "rooms" or "areas" can be created. When changing focus from one product to another, the visual merchandisers can simply rearrange the space to suit the new "narrative." The ceiling grids are wired for electricity so that lighting, video displays, and even the cash/wrap units are all mobile and can be easily rearranged in the space. The IKEA image—light, natural wood, crisp white, and signature colors (yellow and blue)—is ubiquitous throughout. A ramp leads shoppers to the rear of the space where they will encounter the stairway to the upper level. On the mezzanine, the IKEA Cafe serves coffee, cake, Swedish sandwiches, and other specialties.

New York, New York

Designer/Architect: **Walker Group/CNI**
Design Team: **Diego Garay, Derick Hudspith, Steven Kitezh, Patricia Oris, Michael Ross, David Wales, William Wichart, and Renata Zednicek**
Photography: **Dorothée Ahrens**

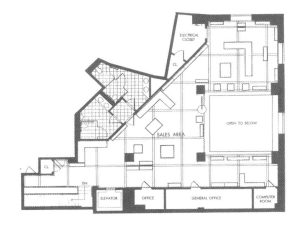

"…the visual

merchandisers

can simply

rearrange

the space to

suit the

new 'narrative.'"

Domain

Domain, a chain of stores featuring high-quality furniture and home accessories, introduced a successful new store design in 1992, which was realized in better malls across the country. In establishing this 7,000-square-foot, freestanding Paramus location, the company called upon the Boston-based firm of Bergmeyer Associates to adapt and enhance that design to cater to a more refined buyer, and to capitalize on the current tendency of consumers to invest in their homes and surroundings.

With more space than a typical mall affords, Domain is organized into a series of homelike vignettes offering shoppers fresh concepts and ideas for furnishing their homes. Much like a wardrober approach, Domain is designed to graphically illustrate how home furnishings and decorative pieces can accessorize a home to suit a particular lifestyle. Depicting distinct home settings like kitchens, bedrooms, and living rooms, the individual vignettes appear within a larger sophisticated and harmonious scheme.

According to the designers, the objective was for space to complement the fashionable furniture it contains without competing with it. The original prototype was high Modern in style, timeless and understated, while the overall context was warm and domestic. To this, designers added panels of stained maple to serve as room dividers and display walls. To coordinate with the furniture, neutral terrazzo was chosen for the floors. The building, which was originally two structures, underwent major changes. A steel-and-glass-front system was added and stone pilasters flank the storefront bay and support the copper overhang. The letters on the signage appear black during the day but are illuminated at night for high visibility. Inside, the bearing wall between the two original structures is now a major display wall, with large, attractive, cut-out openings and portals—affording the creative retailer exciting presentation opportunities.

Paramus, **New Jersey**

Designer: Bergmeyer Associates, Inc.
Principal-in-charge: Joseph P. Nevin, Jr.
Associate-in-charge: Nina Monastero, AIA
Project Manager: Jeanne Carey, AIA

For Domain
Chairman and CEO: Judy George

Photography: Chun Y Lai Photography

"Domain is designed to graphically illustrate how home furnishings

and decorative

pieces can

accessorize a

home to pursue

a particular lifestyle."

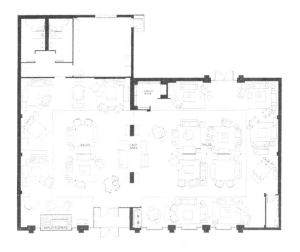

William Ashley China

With this handsome 24,000-square-foot flagship store in Toronto, William Ashley China, Canada's leading retailer of hand-crafted china, crystal, and silverware, appeals to a new larger and younger audience. Once past the granite and glass storefront and the white marble entry, shoppers are enveloped by a welcoming, luxurious interior of warm woods, glowing neutral tones, glass, and soft beige carpeting where they are invited to wander freely through the elegant settings. The large size of the space, as well as the vast array of product lines, led the architect, Christopher Barriscale, to approach the design as if it were "an urban development project." Shoppers travel along centrally located "Gift Avenue," and step off into individual boutiques.

As an alternative solution to the usual glass presentation cases and vitrines, Barriscale designed cylindrical, floor-to-ceiling display towers that also serve to "frame the room." The curved shape is continued through the space in the form of bowed fixtures, sweeping feature walls, and a central "gazebo" topped with an illuminated rotunda—the hub of the layout. Merchandise is displayed on stepped wall shelves, in recessed, self-illuminated shadow boxes, and on counters and in cases with elegant, light wood veneers. As it is three times more transparent than regular glass, Starfire Glass is used throughout. Floor drawers and storage cabinets are incorporated into the open plan, complementing the well-run stock room. While waiting for packages to be delivered, customers are invited to partake of a complimentary Perrier in a crystal goblet, or a cafe-au-lait served on fine china at the Water Bar/Crystal Cafe. The wave-shaped, effervescent, water-filled glass bar provides an "entertainment center for four-year-olds while their parents shop."

Toronto, **Canada**

Designer/Architect: **Christopher Barriscale Architects**
Executive Architects: **International Design Group**
Photography: **Richard Johnson/Interior Images**

"...shoppers are

enveloped by a

welcoming, luxurious

interior of warm

woods, glowing neutral

tones, glass, and soft

beige carpeting."

Robert Dyas
The Ironmongers

England's leading chain of hardware stores for well over a century, Robert Dyas The Ironmongers now has a new look, a new image, and a new presentation of home accessories and hardware to suit the lifestyles of both old and new customers.

This new store, designed by Crabtree Hall/Plan Creatif, respects the heritage of the venerable firm, but places it in a more contemporary context, allowing Dyas to stock and display a vast inventory of products. Continuing a long-standing tradition, tinware is still displayed outside, inviting browsers to rummage and touch, while customers in search of china, glass, appliances, or electrical equipment can find what they want inside. The interior of the store combines old with new. A modern, modular shelving system complements traditional wooden counters; and the oak timber floor, galvanized steel detailing, and painted wood paneling recall and reinforce the look of hardware stores of old. A centrally located cash/wrap desk serves as the hub of the simple layout.

To direct the shopper and draw attention to the assortment of products, the designers have combined basic, linear fluorescent lights with recessed, low-voltage spotlights to highlight featured wall displays. The store graphics, also by Crabtree Hall, add to the comfort and convenience of the shopping experience by helping to quickly locate merchandise and providing information necessary for completing a sale.

Petersfield, **England**

Design: **Crabtree Hall/Plan Creatif**
Partner-in-charge: **David S. Mackay**
Designer: **Paul Mullins**
Photography: **Peter Cook**

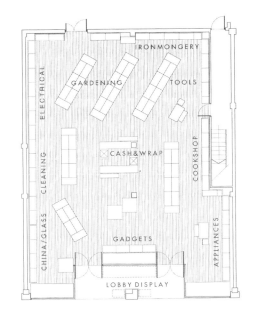

Kitchen Bazaar

There are those of us who cook to live, and those of us who live to cook. But the multi-store chain Kitchen Bazaar exists for the serious cook who considers the culinary arts a basic necessity and way of life. This 5,000-square-foot location was the subject of an intensive replanning, refocusing, and remerchandising operation by Grid/3 International of New York City.

The canopy over the entrance echoes the large, stainless steel hood above the demonstration stove in the central test kitchen area, where classes and events are regularly scheduled. The central aisle leading to the kitchen, as well as some of the smaller aisles, are covered with terra-cotta tiles; the rest of the floor space is neutrally carpeted. Simple black-and-white signage directs customers to specific merchandise and brand-name products, located on the stainless steel shelving units that line the store. Contrasting the cold precision and institutional look of the shelving and signage, rough-hewn pine tables heaped with colorful displays suggest the warmth of home and hearth, as well as add more vibrancy to the store's decor. Near the cash register stations, impulse products are deftly showcased against a white grid background.

Gourmet cookware, tabletop, and bakeware can be found in a specialty boutique just off the central aisle; both international and domestic brands are featured up front. In this well-illuminated and open space, every product is assured an effective showing.

Fort Worth, **Texas**

Design: Grid/3 International
Interior Design: Josefino Borja
Strategy & Merchandise Assortment: Martin Roberts
Graphic Design and Display: Betty Chow
Photography: Craig Kuhner

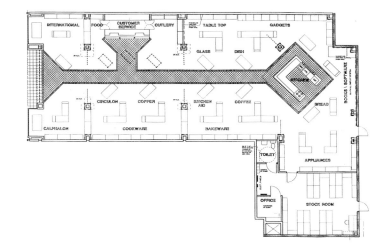

Scott Shuptrine

It's not surprising that an 80,000-square-foot building filled with furniture and home accessories would seem overwhelming to some customers. Charged with transforming the existing structure, Jon Greenberg Associates created a "retailing theater," where customers can comfortably experience the depth and breadth of the store's selection. Rather than encountering a maze of cluttered rooms, shoppers are invited to enjoy lifestyle-specific merchandising presented as designs for total living.

Throughout the store, light and neutral backdrops highlight changing patterns and colors in each of the store's six lifestyle settings. Each grouping is contained on a twenty-six-foot diameter "pod" large enough to show off several rooms of related furniture. The coordinated styles progress naturally and logically from Traditional and Country on the left, to Neo-Classic on the right, to Contemporary Casual in the rear. The overhead lighting and architectural elements are designed to focus on groups of rooms. Unique lifestyle features include a "Home Theater" room, as well as a rustic, furnished log cabin complete with fieldstone fireplace and wood-sheathed walls. Fluorescent tubing hidden behind faux windows suggests natural sunlight.

The spacious, formal vestibule has twin curved stairways that lead shoppers to the second level, where home accessories are displayed in specialty settings. If any doubt remains that the designers haven't thought of everything to provide shoppers with comfort, convenience, and freedom to move about unencumbered, there is a fully equipped and supervised child-care center, entertainment areas, and a hospitality center. On the second level the Laurel Cafe provides self-serve tea and espresso.

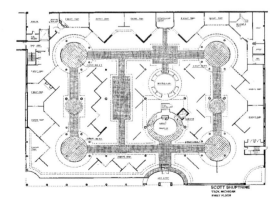

Troy, **Michigan**

Design: **Jon Greenberg Associates**
President: **Ken Nisch**
Photography: **Laszlo Regos Photography**

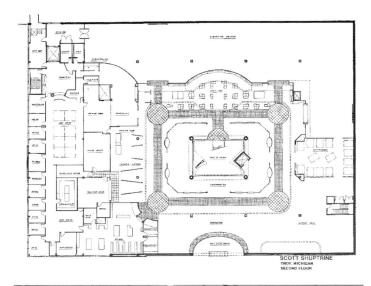

" ... s h o p p e r s   a r e   **invited to enjoy**

lifestyle-specific merchandising..."

Hechinger

This 95,000-square-foot mega-store represents Hechinger's new prototype, which is designed to build on the chain's inherent popularity as the do-it-yourselfer's store of choice, while also offering something for those with a fashion-oriented flair. The convenient layout and strategic, user-friendly plan should appeal to consumers, contractors, and builders alike. An eighteen-foot-wide drive aisle connects the centrally located entrance to a sixteen-foot-wide aisle in the center of the store, allowing every department frontage onto the main aisle while creating a simple, easy-to-understand circulation pattern.

Low fixtures along the aisles offer increased product visibility and the cantilevered warehouse shelving permits viewing from two sides. Off the main aisle, "projects" rather than "products" are displayed in a lifestyle-oriented, residentially-lit Home Decor Center, which is the focal point of the store. The fully accessorized vignette settings provide ideas for creative, lifestyle-conscious home decorating. A color-coded, multi-tiered graphics program increases shoppers' perception of customer service. Signage plays an important role as it directs customers through the store and a specially designed sign system identifies particular brands of products. Other educational signs reinforce value messages, explain home improvement projects—complete with "how-to" diagrams—and list materials necessary to complete specific projects.

Design: Schafer Associates Inc.
Principal-in-charge: Robert W. Schafer
Project Director: Dale Wennlund
Project Designer and Manager: David Koe
Project Architect: Little & Associates
Photography: Bob Briskey, Briskey Photography

42

Laurel, Maryland

Service Center:
HARDWARE CUTTING CENTER

- *we cut screen, glass, plexiglas, chain & rope to size*
- *we cut keys and re-key locksets*
- *we cut high security keys; Medeco, Dom, Kaba & Best*
- *we cut luxury car keys; Lexus, Mercedes, BMW, Saab, etc.*
- *we custom engrave selected products*

"The fully accessorized vignette settings provide ideas for creative, lifestyle-conscious home decorating."

Mega Mart

A visit to the 100,000-square-foot Mega Mart is sure to provide a day's outing for the whole family. Whatever you're looking for, whether it is for the home or the office, if it has anything to do with electronics, computers, software, or appliances, it is sure to be here in a variety of styles, brand names, and price levels. The space is divided into four departments (computer, appliance, electronic, and television and audio) and two main drive aisles, creating an "X" pattern for customer circulation, with a large information center at the intersection. "We wanted the store to be theatrical but with a program and a hierarchy that made sense," says J'Amy Owens, president and creative director of The Retail Group, the design group responsible for this project, which eloquently combines entertainment with retail and a source of wonder with good value.

The computer department, called Computer University, features decorative elements reminiscent of academia: colonnades, a science lab, a stadium, and a library for software. The Mart House, in the appliance area, is fully equipped with General Electric products in place, a whirlpool spa on the deck, and a garden. The header for the television and audio department resembles a big city skyline: skyscrapers and towers are outlined in neon with faux windows that are actually television screens. Bridging the "industrial" and "big city" settings are two Home Theater rooms in the electronics area which feature theater marquees with flashing lights. Each department is specially colorized and the graphics and signage enable customers to move easily and effectively throughout the store. And to delight shoppers of all ages, a Coney Island food court contributes to the flavor of this "snapshot of the American landscape."

Design: The Retail Group
President and Creative Director: J'Amy Owens
Vice President: Christopher Gunter, AIA
Store Planner: Kimberly Bykerk, ASID
Project Manager: Jim Powers
Graphics and Prop Designer: Phil Jones

For Mega Mart, Omaha
President: Ron Blumkin
Chairman: Irv Blumkin
Project Coordinator: Buddy Turner
Associate Architect: Ken Hahn & Associates

Photography: Craig Harrold

Omaha, **Nebraska**

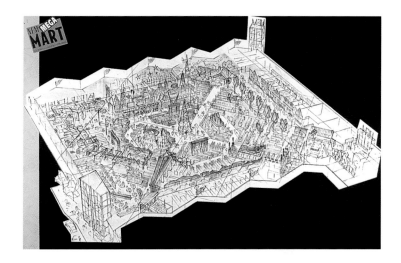

Search for Knowledge

The quest for knowledge makes one's life richer. It allows people who don't have the opportunity to travel extensively to satisfy their **wanderlust**—to fly, sail, see the world, visit past centuries, or glimpse into the future. Reading, visiting museums, going to the theater, and traveling are all activities of a culture driven lifestyle.

To satisfy the desire for knowledge, **bookstores** are *blossoming* all around the world. Not only are they growing in size, they have become literary "department stores," with something for everyone—from young children just learning their ABCs to retired college professors still engrossed in learning. In addition to the **vast**, organized presentation of **reading** mater-ial, many now feature recorded **music**, **computer** software, and gift items. More often than not, a visit to the new bookstore is enhanced by a stop at the in-store cafe, where

customers can **indulge** their **minds** as well as their appetites.

Like the returning traveler who brings home a souvenir of his or her journey, museumgoers also can frequent shops in museums or botanical gardens where tangible memories are for sale. Museum

shops and outposts of fine *arts* museums are now regularly appearing in malls, where people who can purchase reproductions of jewelry and artworks, books, stationery, and home decorations—all based on the fine arts. If knowledge is culture, then a cultured lifestyle is an unending search for knowledge and **self-enrichment**.

Voyagers, The Travel Store

For those with a passion for travel, this prototype store for Voyagers consists of both a travel agency and a travel store. A wide range of books, maps, and globes are offered for sale, along with other travel accessories like compasses and portable alarm clocks. In addition, a knowledgable staff of travel agents is on hand to assist with travel plans, make hotel reservations, and book flights. Both services are comfortably housed together in this 3,600-square-foot space.

A drum-shaped counter, centered on a giant compass and map of the world on the floor, serves as the cash/wrap and information services, where glass cases hold small gift items while the sides of the counter are fitted with shelves for books and larger items. As the hub of the store, the counter divides it into four distinct quadrants: the entry; the travel consultation area; books and maps; and stock. In the center of the drum, a clock tower showcases several timepieces that tell the time in eight major tourist destinations around the world.

Set against such a simple and subdued color palette—gray slate flooring and neutral carpeting to define areas of the floor, and maple trim for the millwork—visual merchandising is highly effective. The floor units, which vary in size and shape, are all readily movable and can be creatively rearranged into various configurations. Fluorescent lighting was chosen for both the concealed light coves and in the recessed ceiling cans because of its economy and "contribution to the overall intimacy" of the store. While most Voyagers customers may already have experienced the "romance of travel," that message is underscored by the canopy over the entrance, which is highly evocative of the steel and glass European railway sheds of the nine-teenth century.

Dallas, Texas

Designer: Michael Malone Architects, Inc.
Principal-in-charge: Michael Malone, AIA
Project Architect: David N. Droese, AIA
Job Captain: Michael Stoddard
Photography: Jud Haggard Photography

"For those

with a passion for travel..."

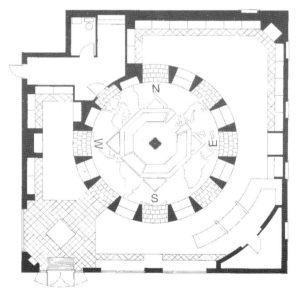

Dillons

In the United States we are seeing a growing number of ever larger mega-bookstores opening, so it should not be a surprise to find a giant 18,000-square-foot, six-story bookstore on New Street in Birmingham, England. Dillons, a growing chain, has successfully transformed an 1865 landmark bank building into a cozy haven for bibliophiles. The London-based design firm Fitch maintained many of the original architectural features, while updating the space to serve both the retailer and the reader.

A fabulous stained-glass, barrel-vaulted roof crowns the central open atrium. The roof was raised sixteen feet to create an arcaded gallery for academic and reference books. Much of the main level is covered by a high, richly coffered ceiling and lined with bookcases, where fiction, travel, and music books are housed. Toward the rear of the floor is a music department stocked with compact discs and cassettes of classical and popular music. In an adjacent reading room, decorated with ornate plaster cornices and refurbished mahogany paneling, customers are welcome to relax, read a newspaper, scan a book, or plug in a conveniently located headset and listen to music.

To reach the first level there is a grand staircase that separates into two sweeping, semi-circular stairways. Art, history, religion, and some nonfiction are found on this level, where you'll also find the bank's original hall clock, now inlaid in the floor. For those seeking children's books or bargains, the lower level is accessed by a feature staircase that leads down to the original flagstone floor. In place of the bank's safes and vaults, the children's department boasts a giant jack-in-the-box, several play tables, and a large-screen video monitor. Woven directly into the custom carpeting in this area are all sorts of floor games for children. Throughout the store traditional tables and chairs provide rest areas for the browser's comfort, convenience, and reading pleasure.

Birmingham, **England**

Design: Fitch
Photography: Tom Blewden, *top*
Chris Hollick, *opposite above and opposite below right*
John Linden, *below and opposite below left*

Children in Paradise

For parents who love books, this bookstore on North Rush Street is the perfect place to bring the kids. Designed especially for children, Children in Paradise is a place where kids are catered to and parents are mere visitors. Children have their own entrance into the 2,500-square-foot store where they are invited to step through a child-size door cut into the full-size door beneath the black canvas canopy bearing the store's name and logo. Adorned with trompe l'oeil paintings of a castle—complete with turrets, casement windows, climbing ivy, clowns, dragons, queens, and kings—the interior is a child's dream come true. The gazebo-like cash/wrap desk in the center has displays below that invite children to touch while parents pay for purchases.

There is an excavated reading pit covered with teal carpet where children can sit or stretch out on the steps, as well as participate in any of the planned activities that are scheduled regularly in the store. For eight- to fourteen-year-old customers, there is a reading loft built with ceilings that range from seven to eighteen feet in height. The winding staircase leading up to the loft is partially obscured by a fanciful arrangement of puppets and stuffed toys. Throughout, the maple-toned bookshelves are self-illuminated and recessed; the books are displayed at a child's eye level and with the illustrated front covers facing forward. This "magical playground" is enchantingly illuminated with incandescent pendants and neon cove lighting in assorted colors.

Chicago, **Illinois**

Design: **Marvin Herman & Associates, Inc.**
Principal: **Marvin Herman**
Project Architects: **Marc Cerone, Michael Vanderpoel**
Decor Team/Muralist: **Cindy Simes, Simes Painting Co.**
Photography: HNK Architectural Photography, Inc.

"Designed especially for children, Children in Paradise is a place where kids are catered to and parents are mere visitors."

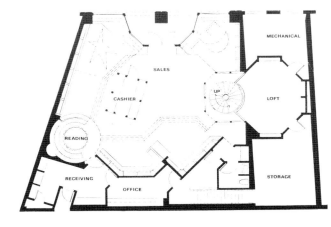

Globe Corner Bookstore

For Bostonians who enjoy traveling around the world, the Globe Corner Bookstore is often the first stop. This 2,000-square-foot store on Bolyston Street specializes in books, maps, and globes—all oriented towards the would-be traveler. Behind the dark green awnings and bay windows, the shop is divided into a gallery and a map room, with a cash/wrap desk strategically located between them, beneath a dropped ceiling. Globes are used as props in the windows, at the cash/wrap station, and are prominently displayed in the map room. The thirteen-foot ceilings in the two rooms allow for a wide soffit around the perimeter for the presentation of maps and charts, which are effectively displayed by means of a Shaker-style peg-hanging system. The removable pegs and crossbars grip the maps at the top and bottom, and can adjust to a variety of sizes.

The natural wood bookcase units in both rooms have adjustable shelves and are self-illuminated. A stepped fixture was also designed to integrate the numerous resource materials and to display smaller items. The walls and the soffit are painted a warm beige; two different shades of gray carpeting define specific areas in the store. Track lighting is used in combination with recessed cans with incandescent lamps in the dropped ceilings. Custom designed, spherical lighting fixtures not only illuminate the space but serve to subliminally reinforce the idea of world travel.

Boston, Massachusetts

Design: Bergmeyer Associates, Inc.
Principal: Robert M. Wood, AIA
Decorator: Christine Canning
Job Captain: Matthew Hyatt
Project Manager: Dan Anderson
Graphic Design: Victoria Blaine Design
Photography: Lucy Chen Photography

Museum
of Fine Arts, Boston

Art lovers and other people who visit museums often long to bring some small piece of beauty back home with them. To help satisfy this desire, the Museum of Fine Arts, Boston has opened its first off-site retail store. This 2,300-square-foot space in the Mall at Chestnut Hill offers an eclectic sampling of the museum's treasures—in reproduction, of course—to those who cherish the aesthetics of art and the finer things in life.

With its "crisp, undiluted Federal style Neo-Classicism," the facade recalls the finest in New England architectural traditions. The slender pilasters and the visual transparency of the design allow clear sight lines to the interior. The museum-like presentation is featured prominently in the signature white millwork and balanced with natural cherry wood and antique brass. The high walls are painted a warmer white and the carpeting is neutral. The simple but versatile custom casework wall system is articulated by bay-like projections that divide categories of merchandise. The wall cases have adjustable glass shelves and fabric-covered back panels. An occasional cherry wood feature wall interrupts the procession of cases, and low storage drawers allow for some storage on the floor.

The floor fixtures include movable open tables and glass-topped cases—focal islands in the store where the museum's jewelry reproductions are showcased. In an elegant presentation similar to that of an art gallery, framed prints are displayed in the rear.

Chestnut Hill, **Massachusetts**

Architect/Design: **Bergmeyer Associates, Inc.**
Principal-in-charge: **Joseph P. Nevin, Jr.**
Project Manager: **Ross Cromarty**

For the Museum of Fine Arts, Boston
General Manager: **Janet Emerson**
Director of Stores: **Jeffrey Shoup**
Product Developing/Merchandise Manager: **Cynthia Palmer**

Photography: **Lucy Chen Photography**

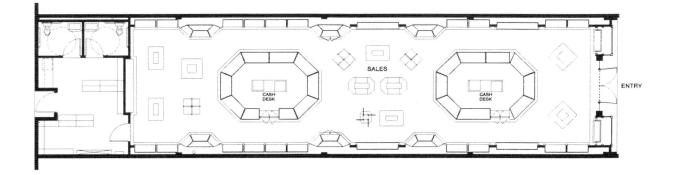

Detroit Institute of Arts Museum Shop

A fourteen-foot-high Ionic colonnade separates this museum satellite shop into two distinct settings that represent both indoors and outdoors. Though physically removed from the historic museum on Woodward Street in Detroit, the arched entrance of that building was the inspiration for the colonnade, which beautifully simulates weathered limestone. Avid museumgoers and people who want to bring the aesthetics of the past into their lives and homes can shop here for reproductions of artwork, jewelry, books, framed prints, and other items.

Natural toned granite tile on the floors and faux stone wall coverings define the "outdoor" area, where high ceilings provide spaciousness to the miniature statuary of reproductions. Replicas of artworks hang on the walls, while solid mahogany jewelry cases—accented with strips of pewter and highlighted with tall display towers—connect the two spaces and subtly lead shoppers back and forth between them.

In the rear of the "indoor" space, colorful inlaid tile in the image of a compass is set into the floor, a replica of the original mosaic in the Detroit Institute of Art's Rivera Court, where Diego Rivera's giant mural, *Detroit Industry*, covers four entire walls. A detail from that mural is displayed above the compass medallion, where the main bookcase units curve around to it. Custom-fabricated of mahogany, all of the bookcases are equipped with totally adjustable shelves. Custom-curved, shelved floor units display children's merchandise and museum T-shirts. Posters, framed art, and stained-glass items are shown on backlit panels, flip pages, and stepped fixtures at the rear of the store. Throughout, the designers have chosen highly textural and subliminal lighting with recessed ceiling fixtures and cove-hidden tracks.

Novi, **Michigan**

Design: Jon Greenberg & Associates (JGA)
Principal-in-charge: Kenneth Nisch
Project Manager: Michael Curtis
Project Designer: Elaine Albers
Director of Creative Resources: Tony Camilletti
Executive Director of Professional Services: Gregory Geralds
Photography: Laszlo Regos Photography

"In the rear of the 'indoor' space, colorful inlaid tile in the image of a compass is set into the floor..."

Gallerie Lassen

If you long for the sea but live nowhere near it or have no way to get there, the next best way to bring the sea into your life is to bring it into your home. The new 6,000-square-foot flagship Gallerie Lassen, located in the Forum Shops in land-locked Las Vegas, was designed to help make that dream come true. The gallery is filled with seascapes and underwater scenes painted by the marine artist Christian Riese Lassen. A grand, sweeping staircase connects the main level to the mezzanine; the illuminated handrail was carved by the glass artist John Garafolo. Paintings and sculpture are displayed on the spacious landings, and the life-size dolphins frisking about in the dome overhead are the work of the sculptor Doug Wylie. The dome is the centerpoint in the ceiling design of stepped, neon-lit coves.

Sculptural in concept, the lush space is rendered in Texas shell limestone, stamped concrete, carved and etched glass, and perforated metal panels accented by the cool, marine palette of greens and blues. The freestanding walls are clad with patinaed copper with shell limestone wainscoting. The "island" feeling is further enhanced by images of palm fronds and tropical foliage projected onto the ceiling. Up front, a large cylindrical aquarium draws shoppers' attention and a wall-size video monitor pictures the featured artist, Lassen, at work and at play (in the water, of course) in his native Hawaii.

Las Vegas, **Nevada**

Designer/Architect: Brand & Allen Architects
Project Architects: Steve Lochte and Gary McCartney
Lighting Effects: Luminae Souter
Photography: Jud Haggard Photography

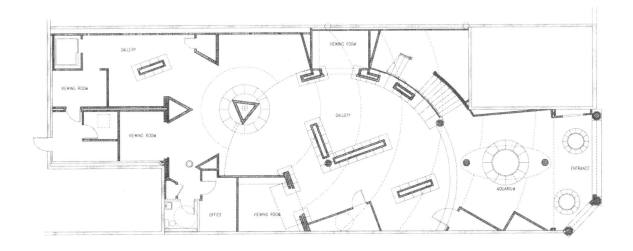

The Garden Shop of the Chicago Botanic Garden

The new Garden Shop at the Chicago Botanic Garden is a vital part of the 16,500-square-foot Gateway Center. It is here that visitors can find the books, bulbs, and souvenirs that will enhance their visit to the gardens and their memories of it. The recently expanded shop now offers more products in a warm and natural space that is practically a continuation of the gardens themselves, which it overlooks. To fill the lofty space, the design concept calls for elements and fixtures made primarily of wood. White panels accented with clear lacquered wood dowels and molding strips are integrated with natural wood wall constructions and overhanging wooden trellises that help to define specific areas of the store. The design firm, Eva Maddox Associates of Chicago, was also responsive to the problems of maintenance in the heavily trafficked facility and approached the project with a sensitive, quality orientation to provide cost-effective design. In keeping with its setting, the lighting plan accommodates, complements, and enhances natural daylight by its careful choice of lighting fixtures and lamps. Track lights, recessed fixtures, and indirect illumination are all combined to achieve a natural, sunny, outdoors ambience.

Chicago, Illinois

Design: Eva Maddox Associates
President and Creative Director: Eva L. Maddox
Vice President, Director of Design: Eileen Jones
Project Designers: Keith Curtis, Julie Kruer-Doyle,
     Marybeth Rampolla
Senior Vice President, Lighting and Technical Specialist:
     Patrick H. Grzybek
Retail Specialist: Kathy S. Vierra
Photography: Steve Hall, Hedrich-Blessing

"The recently expanded shop now offers more products in a warm and natural space that is practically a continuation of the gardens themselves…"

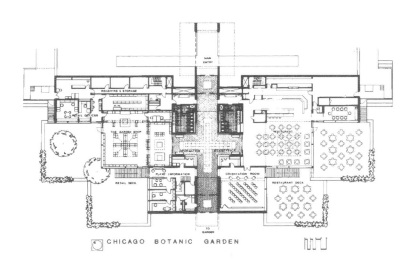

CHICAGO BOTANIC GARDEN

Discovery Channel Store

Intended for the more than 75 million people who watch the Discovery Channel on cable television, this unique store will satisfy any customer who thirsts for knowledge or who is stimulated by educational television programming. If you fear you have missed a particular program of interest, many are available here on video, and CD-ROM; computer software that reinforces the programming can also be found. Because the 2,700-square-foot store is situated in an 1895 landmark building, the historic columns, crown and base moldings, and antique storefront were required to be maintained. There was also a restriction against the use of lighting or any construction being attached directly to the walls or the barrel vaulted ceilings.

The store is divided into areas of interest such as Gardening and the Outdoors; Geology and Fossils; Weather and Astronomy; Science and Nature; Nature Photography; and Children's Toys, Books, and Games. Freestanding light towers not only help to divide the space, but draw attention to the nineteen-foot-high ceilings. The tower tops contain indirect lighting and tracks which can be trained on particular floor displays. The main wall units located between the towers are equipped with fluorescents. In line with the store's commitment to the environment, no rain forest hardwoods have been used. All of the light towers, wall fixtures, and floor fixtures are trimmed with natural wood moldings over a plastic laminate. The slate flooring at the entrance yields to blue-green, vegetable-dyed carpeting; the existing historic walls and ceilings are painted a warm beige. The storefront was adapted with the use of period-correct gold leaf signs and logos, and an antique, cast-iron sign boom was fitted with a new sign.

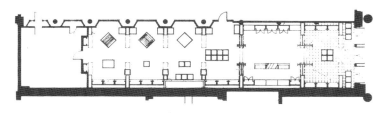

Galveston, **Texas**

Designer/Architect: Michael Malone Architects, Inc.
Principal-in-charge: Michael Malone, AIA
Project Manager: Michael Stoddard
Photography: Jud Haggard Photography

UCLA Spirit

One of the more educated choices for souvenir shoppers along touristy Universal Citywalk is the UCLA Spirit shop, which brings the essence of campus life—both past and present—to the larger community. Like the other retail spaces surrounding it, UCLA Spirit is a dynamic mix of state-of-the-art technology and nostalgia. The rust-colored Romanesque arches of the facade are reminiscent of UCLA's nineteenth-century Royce Hall, but they take on an entirely new meaning in their present context: a twenty-seven-foot tall, blue and yellow neon-outlined tower with a rotating bruin's head on top.

Inside, the Romanesque inspiration continues with arches, sculptured details, warm terra-cotta-colored bricks, and gold tinted limestone. The university colors, yellow and blue, are used as decorative accents throughout and appear time and again on the logo products and apparel. The giant bear pawprint, cast in the entrance floor, sets the theme for the meandering floor plan. There is a mosaic of ceramic tiles fired with texts and images from old UCLA yearbooks and student newspapers. A wall of video screens adds a more contemporary note.

The wall units, for shelved as well as hung apparel, are made of wood and amusingly stylized with arched colonnades, pedimented tops, and columns—all reflecting the architecture and art of the UCLA campus. The featured merchandise is the "Bearwear," specifically designed for this shop. In addition to textbooks and supplies for UCLA students, customers can take home a piece of UCLA tradition in the form of T-shirts, sweats, hats, and other apparel for the whole family, as well as tote bags, backpacks, stuffed bears, and even jewelry.

Universal City, **California**

Design: ASUCLA
Store Design, Graphics, Packaging: **Steven Kelso, Phyllis Schultz**
Mosaics: **69th Street West Ceramic Design**
Murals: **Rufus Snoddy**
Photography: ASUCLA

British Columbia & Beyond

People who travel are often collectors. Like museumgoers, they may collect postcards, snow scenes captured under glass, or the local arts and crafts of the places they have visited. British Columbia & Beyond, located in the Vancouver International Airport, provides visitors with a final opportunity before flying away to find just the right memento or souvenir of their journey.

Upon entering, the store appears much larger than its 1,320 square feet, and is finished in the characteristic textures and colors of British Columbia. The Squamish rock that faces the interior and exterior columns, for instance, is also used as a partial fascia on the service desk. The stonework not only adds a sense of stability and tranquility to the space, but serves as a natural habitat for the presentation of local products and artwork.

As a soothing contrast, clear maple millwork and porcelain and wood floors are highly effective against the stone. The two-sided fixtures that serve as the window displayers are made up of carved maple logs, as is the distressed timber framework of the service desk. For contrast with the earth tones, warm shades of purple are introduced on the ceiling and the wall trim.

An "open cabinet" approach was taken for the wall display as it allows products to be featured in a narrative fashion and provides visual relief to the overall presentation. Finally, suspended maple signage beautifully augments the departments and simplifies the shopping experience for customers who are in a hurry to catch their plane.

Vancouver International Airport,
British Columbia, **Canada**

Design: Sunderland Innerspace Design, Inc.
Design Team: Jonathan McNeely, Janice McAllister,
Jon Sunderland
Visual Displays: Everett Elizade, Host Marriott Corp.
Photography: Rob Melnychuk Photography

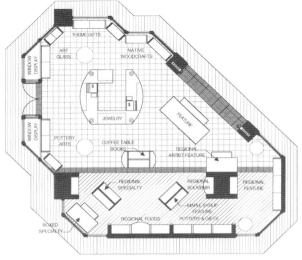

"...a final opportunity

...**to find just** the right memento..."

The Living is Easy

Today, taking it easy means doing it in style. Fortunately, there are countless ways to dress down and relax—it all depends on your **lifestyle attitude**. Perhaps your ecologically-conscious style means getting back to nature and the basics. Or it could be a reflection of an all-American heritage, a sense of tradition that dictates a style, perhaps represented by the LA, **laid back**, Southern California way of life. Button-down Oxford shirts and penny loafers still evoke the "preppy" lifestyle, and though tennis whites are right for the tennis court, they can also double as the perfect outfit to wear to **relax**—in a very upscale way. It used to be that jeans were just rough, rather styleless, blue denim pants that were considered work clothes. Today, the ubiquitous pair of jeans are a major contemporary fashion statement available in an infinite variety of **fits**, **sizes**, and **colors**, plus a little something special added to the traditional jeans design by each manufacturer to attract laid back lifestylers.

Communing with nature also calls for special clothes. Companies like Eddie Bauer and The North Face cater to the nature loving lifestyle with clothes, accessories, and even home furnishings to complete a domestic envi-

ronment in keeping with that lifestyle. Ordinary nine-to-fivers can become weekend cowboys, cowgirls, and ranch hands at Out of the West, which brings the wild west to Chicago, where customers can purchase hats, boots, belts, and buckles—as well

as the appropriate baubles and bangles. This store also features home furnishings that can transform an apartment on Lake Shore Drive into a hunting lodge in Montana. The living may be easy, but you still have to **dress for it**.

Original Levi's Store

Blue jeans—the most popular American clothing—
have become almost synonymous with Levi's. Traditionally targeted
for a core group of customers between the ages of sixteen and twenty-
four, the Levi's market has considerably expanded to include this core
group's parents and grandparents, which proves that the comfortable,
blue jeans lifestyle has no age limit. To design their flagship Original
Levi's Store in midtown Manhattan, the company selected Boston-
based Bergmeyer Associates, Inc., to fashion an exciting retail environment within this 15,000-square-foot, four-level space.

A large atrium unifies all four levels of the store, which are connected by stairways and an elevator, while open spaces between areas
allow for moments of activity throughout the entire space. Interactive
kiosks provide information in four languages to help both international and native shoppers find whatever it is they want. Large-scale
trompe l'oeil murals, a history wall, and heritage graphics reinforce
the image and quality of the Levi's brand name. The overall state-of-
the-art, multimedia experience that this lifestyle espouses is further
enhanced by large-screen, rear projected videos with integrated sound
that fill all four levels. Eight-foot-tall video screens are located on the
first two levels; smaller monitors take over on the upper two levels.

Each level houses a specific portion of the Levi's World: the
most fashionable products are introduced on the main floor; Levi's
Shoes, a new addition, is on the mezzanine; Levi's Red Tab and
501 assortments have their own floor; as does apparel for women,
which includes a custom-fit jeans department. To underscore this
casual feeling, North American maple—either a cherry color or
stained gray or black—is used for the fixtures and trim throughout.
Ubiquitous maple display fixtures rise from floor to ceiling, and the
Scandinavian beech floor is inlaid with red stripes, contributing a
warm accent to the friendly ambiance.

New York, New York

Designer/Architect: Bergmeyer Associates, Inc.
Principal-in-charge: Joseph P. Nevin, Jr.
Project Manager: Daniel Broggi, R.A.
Photography: Chun Y Lai Photography

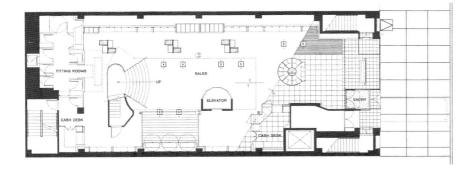

"Each level houses **a specific portion**

Guess?

Though Guess itself asks the question, it also provides all the right answers for those who want a wardrobe to harmonize with their casual lifestyle. Indeed, the Guess lifestyle is the denim lifestyle: the carefree, easygoing American lifestyle. To achieve that look for its Boston location, Guess pays homage to American architecture and sensibilities in a contemporary, unexpected way. According to Judith Winchester, the company's director of visual merchandising, "We built a beautiful store that's fun, but still consistent with sophisticated Newbury Street architecture."

Dramatic presentations fill the many windows and denim is a strong presence on the wall opposite the entrance, immediately bespeaking the Guess lifestyle. Inside, the two-level, 8,400-square-foot space, which was once a bank, is filled with textures, colors, and memorabilia that powerfully evoke the American Heartland. There are old-fashioned storefronts, newspaper stands, bins of grain, and wicker baskets that support and display the merchandise. The Mission and Shaker influences are apparent in the wood fixtures, and the use of all-American fabrics like gingham, ticking, and denim to cover the busts on the "antique" iron bases, adds to a feeling of nostalgia. The wood floors, neutral coloring, and high coffered ceiling contribute to the warm, homey style.

The main level consists primarily of women's jeans, shoes, and casual business attire. Displays clustered around the angled staircase leading to the mezzanine introduce the men's fashions, which are located upstairs. Though Guess has always been a strong presence on the West Coast, this new store design and concept celebrates the Guess sensibilities of diversity, abundance, and comfort, illustrating quite clearly that Guess is ready to take on an East Coast lifestyle image as well.

Boston, **Massachusetts**

Design: **Guess In-House**
Architect/Designer: **Geert De Turek**
Director of Visual Merchandising: **Judith Winchester/Designer**
Architect: **Gunderson**
Photography: **Andrew Bordwin**

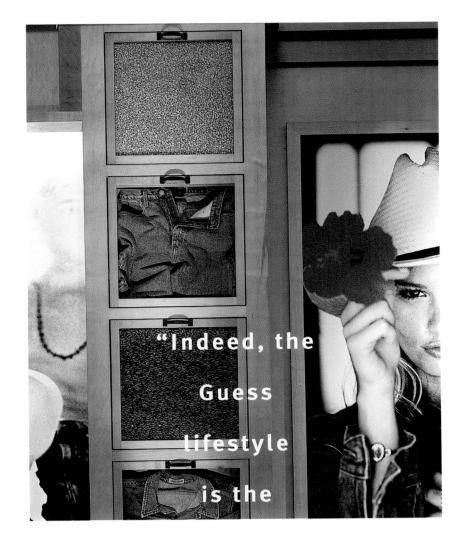

"Indeed, the Guess lifestyle is the denim lifestyle: the carefree, easygoing American lifestyle."

Fitigues

Fitigues is more than just a play on the word fatigues, it is lifestyle dressing personified. Aimed at the fit and the vigorous, Fitigues carries only truly casual and relaxed clothing for the family that works out. By stripping layers of plaster from the early-twentieth-century building, the designer, Harry Swihart, exposed the original brick, revealing "a history of infilled windows and wood lintels still in place." The irregular shape of the space was used to define men's, women's, and children's merchandising areas. The gypsum ceiling, which is required by law, is enlivened by trim that echoes the concentric patterns in the new wood floor. Variations in the hand-painted, custom finishes on the ceiling creates the illusion of different heights, helping to delineate the merchandising sections below.

For additional sparkle, galvanized steel spiral ducts and pendant fixtures have been installed, further enhancing the designer's concept of "exposed, natural finishes." Track lighting is aligned so that it coincides with the trim patterns of both floor and ceiling. The designer specified a merchandising system of aluminum pipes and alloy fittings, with shelving of medium density fiberboard. Bolts, threaded into the pipes, serve as accessory displayers and there are pipe face-outs for feature presentations. This system looks natural and allows flexibility in merchandising as well as fixture profiles, as the hanging heights are fully adjustable.

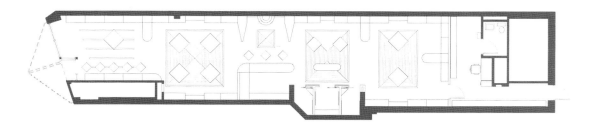

Chicago, **Illinois**

Designer/Architect: **Harry Swihart**
Photography: Steinkamp Ballogg

Old Navy Clothing Company

The family that plays together and lazes together not only stays together but can shop together in the new Old Navy Clothing Company flagship store on Sixth Avenue in New York City. The comfortable, warehouse-like interior is introduced through the metal window system of the facade of this restored, century-old, terra-cotta building. The "glowing marquis has a nostalgic feeling recalling old movie theaters." With a moving track system similar to those used in commercial dry cleaners, the display team introduces Old Navy products in an exciting, kinetic way.

The two floors are connected by escalators located in the center of the store. Old, reclaimed wood floors, bare concrete, exposed brick walls and brick-clad columns, and revealed ductwork all add to the casual, relaxed feeling of Old Navy. Halophane lamps, "jelly-jar" lamps, plus track lights provide a warm glow to the merchandise presentation on the main level. Daylight streams in through a 35-foot by 45-foot skylight on the second level.

The bazaar-like environment and the many references to the past make the store fun to shop in. For example, an open dairy case displays shrink wrapped T-shirts. Accessories and logo items are displayed on a butcher's meat rack above. Bushel baskets are juxtaposed with rough wood pallets for easy visual merchandising, and part of an old bus becomes a focal point and trading center in the children's area. Floor-to-ceiling industrial shelving units display products in vertical color ranges or in coordinated groupings. Steel racks on wheels serve as free-standing floor fixtures. And when a break is needed from shopping, there is a friendly cafe located under the skylight on the upper level.

According to the designers, the challenge was to create an interior that felt as old as the building's exterior. With their eclectic choices of materials, textures, and decorative elements Old Navy succeeds in evoking a classic, timeworn motif.

New York, **New York**

Design: The GAP In-House
Project Designers: Julie Brown, Mark Dvorak
Project Architects: Norman Sears, Steve Sebastian
Visual Merchandising: Jody Patraka, John Valdivia
Photography: Edi Ignacio

OLD NAVY KIDS

OLD NAVY baby

★ IT'S TOUGH STUFF ★   ★ OLD NAVY BABY • START 'EM OUT HERE

"The bazaar-like

environment and the

many references

to the past make

the store fun to

shop in."

Lacoste Boutique

For those with an active lifestyle who are conscious of designer labels and imported brands of merchandise, the Lacoste Boutique, though small, is a precious find. Here, amid other upscale, designer boutiques in the Bal Harbour Shops, Lacoste appeals to its own special brand of client—a suntanned tennis player, for instance. The design of the space is simple and the concept had already been established. As per the standard in every Lacoste Boutique worldwide, all of the display furniture was pre-manufactured and shipped from France.

The colors are natural and neutral. The green of the carpet is the exact color of grass tennis courts and the wood floor blends with the woods of the floor fixtures. The clean white of the walls and ceiling enlarge the space and make colorful merchandise appear more vibrant and attractive. Though all of the lighting fixtures were adapted to meet U.S. standards, they were selected because they most closely matched the lighting fixtures in the Lacoste shops in France. Framed black-and-white photographs of a young M. Lacoste playing tennis are employed as part of the store's decor, appearing on the dropped soffit surrounding the retail space. The pure refinement of the design and the excellent visual merchandising make shopping a pleasurable experience and exemplify the simplicity and elegance of Lacoste designs.

Design: *After Designs by M. Lacoste, France*
Architect: Ralph Choeff Architect, PA.
Contractor: RCC Associates, Inc.
Photography: John Stillman

Bal Harbour, **Florida**

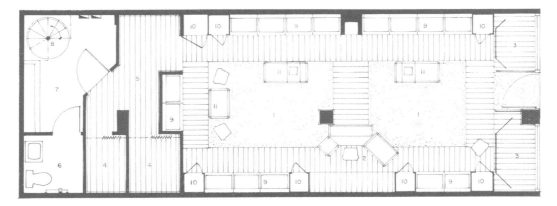

The Bottler's Shop

The younger set in Santiago is usually drawn to most things American, which it finds to be fashion forward. Realizing the universal popularity and instantaneous name recognition of Coca-Cola, Jaime Link commissioned designer Roberto Dannemann of Iceberg Limitada to create an oasis of Americana in the Alto Las Condes Mall, where the young can purchase a variety of clothing and products emblazoned with the famous Coca-Cola logo.

To create the desired retro look, Dannemann drew inspiration from the classic American diners of the 1950s and 1960s, but resisted emphasizing strident colors in favor of restoring the shine of metal combined with the nobility of wood in an overall neutral setting. The highlight of the store is the cash/wrap counter, which recalls a vintage soda fountain of the 1950s, complete with chrome stools topped with red vinyl upholstery. The counter is made of particle board faced with a hard, black ceramic finish. Red and white ceramic tiles form a checkerboard pattern on the floor.

Around the perimeter, a natural wood valance extends from the walls, hiding a white neon border light. Halogen spots are embedded in the valance and are trained on shelving areas which are topped with chrome racks. To counteract the light absorption of the dark colors and woods, metal halide lamps provide general illumination. The fixtures and fittings are all natural wood accented with stainless steel and with aluminum moldings more customary on automobiles.

The design echoes Coca-Cola's logo colors by incorporating a red and white checkered pattern as a baseboard trim on some of the perimeter walls. The ubiquitous presence of the soft drink is further enhanced by a cooler full of Cokes, large-scale Dura-Trans photos, and a video monitor. The diner motif is reinforced by a working jukebox that makes the space both lively and interactive.

Designer: Roberto Dannemann
Production: Iceberg Limitada
Photography: Marcella Castello

"The diner motif is reinforced by a working jukebox that makes the space both

lively and interactive."

Eddie Bauer

For many shoppers, Eddie Bauer typifies a lifestyle rooted in the nature of the great outdoors of the West Coast. To further that image in this new 28,600-square-foot flagship store on San Francisco's Union Square, the designers of FRCH Design Worldwide have filled it with natural raw materials, including assorted woods and stones associated with the Pacific Northwest, along with metal and leather details.

While the original exterior of this turn-of-the-century building was restored to its former look, the interior was completely gutted and reconstructed. Central to the design is a four-story atrium with clerestory lighting, escalators, and massive, handcrafted, iron work chandeliers. The atrium and its decorative elements add the drama of scale and space, and provide customers with clear sightlines to all levels. Large, back-lit graphics of West Coast landscapes underscore the enduring Eddie Bauer lifestyle image.

Each department is tailored to specific merchandise classifications. Traditional design elements create a residential setting for the home products on the lower level, while a rustic setting reminiscent of a bygone era classifies the Sports Shop on the main level. Nearby, Men's Sportswear is displayed in a more refined and contemporary environment, where smooth wood columns and an oak floor contrast to the rough wood and antique pine in the Sports Shop. Subtle grained, hand-rubbed woods and brushed metal appear on the second level, where Women's Sportswear, AKA Eddie Bauer, footwear, and accessories are located. Cotton webbing wall dividers suggest separation without total obstruction. The combination of these elements in one cohesive environment has a synergistic effect as it promotes a casual lifestyle appropriate to each of its merchandise classifications.

Design: FRCH Design Worldwide
Vice President of Design: Barb Fabing
Vice President of Production: Tom Horwitz
Senior Designer: Terri Altenau
Project Architect: Tony Nasser
Designer: Jason Watts

For Eddie Bauer
Director of Store Design: Mike Miller
Director of Visual Presentation: Joe Stoneburner
Project Manager, Design: Norm Johnson
Project Manager, Construction: Joe Scheiner
Manager, Store Planning and Construction: Kevin Gysler

Photography: Paul Bielenberg

San Francisco, **California**

" ...a lifestyle rooted in the

ature of the great outdoors..."

Out of the West

For all those urban cowboys and cowgirls who will most likely never get closer to a steer than when eating a steak, Out of the West has become a sort of "home on West Armitage." In an upscale location, this store sells western clothes, accessories, and home decorations to "country-western wanna-bes."

As it is women who make approximately eighty percent of the purchases here, the designers of this 3,500-square-foot, ground-floor space in a Victorian Chicago apartment building wanted it to be comfortable, warm, and user-friendly, though rough and rustic. The textures, finishes, and colors that would add the most to the ambiance were researched and selected based on Chicago's own Victorian history. Logs and stones were imported from Wyoming and many of the fixtures and decorative elements are old items that have been reworked and adapted to new uses.

Upon entering the store, shoppers are met with a display of western boots on glass shelves that are supported by five-foot-tall, carved wooden totem poles. Some of the walls are covered with split logs mortared together, while others are paved with old bricks. Slabs of rough wood serve as rustic-looking shelving, and the natural wood floor is laid diagonally. Towards the rear of the store, a fieldstone fireplace set into a spruce log mortared wall becomes a hunting or fishing lodge where home fashions are displayed in a lifestyle setting. The versatile fixtures by 555M that appear throughout are constructed of two-by-fours, steel rods, and plank wood shelves. Revitalized old display cases and furniture all add to the look of this truly atmospheric shop. According to co-owner Maureen Reaney, "Western fashions and products become trendy from time to time, but the American fascination with the West is one of the most enduring themes of our culture."

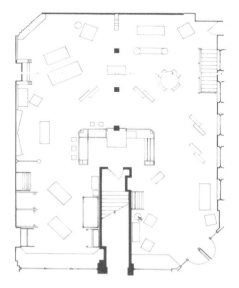

Chicago, **Illinois**

Design: 555 DFM
Principal-in-charge: James Geier
Project Coordinator: Rick Marohn, AIA
Project Architect: Brad Schoch, AIA
Retailers: Bob Gifford, Maureen Reaney
Photography: Peter Williamson, Senior Designer 555 DFM

WH Smith

The goal of the design firm AM Partners in designing this new prototype store for WH Smith was to "do something romantic, to create a shopping experience where people feel they are buying a piece of the place they are in and taking it home with them." More than a "sundry" or "convenience" shop in a resort hotel, this store is designed to be an integral part of the memories of those whose lifestyles involve exotic travel.

Intentionally created to set the stage for the resort locale and to bring local color and flavor to the retailing concept, this 4,700-square-foot space is targeted at the sophisticated traveler, and offers beach- and resort-wear, as well as assorted sundries. Colorful flooring tile, wood moldings, and wood turnings that replicate the balconies and balustrades of Old San Juan all add to the "old world charm" of the design. Designed to replicate an actual house, with a living room, porch, and courtyard, the shop echoes the area's characteristic Spanish Colonial architecture.

Each department of the store is devoted to a particular merchandise category. Passing beneath an arch in a heavily textured, Spanish-style wall, shoppers enter via the patio, which doubles as the menswear section. A trellis-like structure represents an open porch and, above it, the sky blue ceiling is embellished with painted stars. The women's department is more formal and refined, with custom millwork and gilded moldings that recall an elegant living room. In contrast, the children's department, located in the courtyard, is filled with light, color, and the vivacity of the Caribbean setting: sparkling blue water, verdant foliage, and the brilliant reds and oranges of a tropical sunset.

Design: **AM Partners**
President: Charles Lau, AIA
Photography: Andrew Bordwin

Las Croabas, **Puerto Rico**

"...a shopping experience where peopl

"eel they are buying a piece of the place."

Sporting Life

This chapter is devoted to the sporting goods and sportswear stores that cater to both the **fit** and fitness trade and to sports **enthusiasts**. Included are some of

the new mega sports stores that carry top brand names in special boutiques, as well as stores that feature only their own brand of merchandise. There are some that offer shoppers the opportunity to **swing** golf clubs on a green, **shoot** baskets while getting a feel for the ball, *climb* a wall, **ski** on a treadmill, or maybe even set up a tent. Beyond the clothes and the equipment, the sports shopping experience is one of **indulgence** and satisfaction.

Someone who can't find time to buy a new suit for work will spend **hours** gripping golf clubs, checking the finish on skis or snowboards, even agonizing over the color. **Interaction**, shopper **participation**, and keeping the shopper interested until he or she becomes a customer is what sporting lifestyle retail is all about.

Herman's

For **sports enthusiasts** or people with active lifestyles, Herman's, which identifies itself as "The Sports Store of New York," has long been synonymous with selection and value. With its new, 15,600-square-foot, two-story location in Rockefeller Center, Herman's now also stands for entertainment and excitement. The store is filled with quotes from sports greats, mural graphics, and dramatic signage. Information is conveyed on large-screen video monitors, which enhance the drama of this already visually stimulating retail space.

James Mansour, Ltd. designed many unique fixtures, like the wooden gondolas with slotting and the anthracite metal outriggers that are used on the wall system. One of the focal points in the store is the fluted cash/wrap counter, which is finished with marble that is complemented by columns also finished with fluting and graphics panels on all four sides. A nostalgic memorabilia rotunda also draws attention.

To achieve a sophisticated yet sports-oriented ambiance, which plays up its location in Rockefeller Center, the designers did surprising things with the terrazzo, custom carpeting, and cherry wood flooring. Cherry wood veneer also finishes particular walls and fixtures, like the revolving skate displayer. Anthracite hardware is used on floor and wall fixtures. Throughout, the store is designed with special display and interactive visual merchandising presentations, including mannequins that show off complete sportswear ensembles and bas relief panels depicting sporting activities. There are also seasonal promotions with some of the major vendors in the store, such as Nike, Reebok, and Adidas.

New York, **New York**

Design: James Mansour, Ltd.
Project Team: William Koo, James Mansour, Manon Zinzell
Project Architect: Christopher Barriscale Architect
Photography: Antoine Bootz

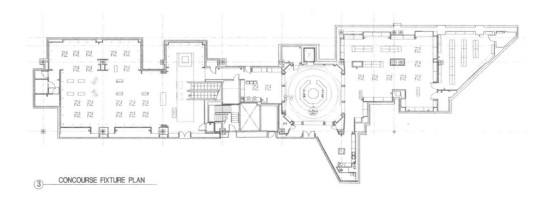

③ CONCOURSE FIXTURE PLAN

"... the store is designed with special display

and interactive

visual merchandising

presentations, including

mannequins that

show off

complete sportswear

ensembles..."

Oshman's SuperSports U.S.A.

"Play before you pay" seems to be the slogan of this store, which is designed to appeal to a broad range of lifestyle shoppers, whether they are golfers, climbers, runners, or just general outdoors people. The 85,000-square-foot space is pure entertainment. Shoppers are invited to walk along the drive aisle track and step off into specialized sports areas, many of which feature unique try-out "fields" where equipment can be tested before being purchased. These include putting greens, regulation and miniature basketball courts, a boxing ring, and a batting cage with an automatic pitching machine. There are also tennis and racquetball courts, a fifty-foot archery range, and a gravity operated rock climbing simulator.

Shoppers' attention is specifically directed toward the visual presentation of key brands. Mannequin displays help to distinguish the Fitness, Athletic Shoes, and Nike Shop areas. A multitiered platform leads customers into an interior zone, where shops are identified by floating ceilings dropped from a twenty-two-foot-high deck. Some of the newer specialty shops include Jake's, a snowboard shop with corrugated metal walls and pipe fixture system; Casual Footwear, a rugged department with timber and laminate granite insets; and Hunting & Camping, an area dominated by a one-hundred-foot-long tent ledge with realistic outdoors vignettes.

Auburn, **Washington**

In-House Planning and Design Team:
Director of Creative Services and Visual Merchandising:
    RoxAnna A. Sway, ISP
Director of Store Planning and Construction: Chris Lauritzen
Project Manager: Bob McBrinn
Visual Merchandising Corporate Coordinators: Nabs Carlson,
    Reggie Gray

Architects: Feola Carli Archuleta Architects
Principal-in-charge: Andrew Feola, AIA
Store Planning/Manager: Luis Cota, ISP
Project Team: Wesley Ashley, AIA, Gisela Riobueno

Photography: Chris Leavitt Photography

The Finish Line

For **many,** the sporting life begins with the proper sports shoes. The Finish Line is a store with a wide range of footwear for sports enthusiasts. The store's layout and ambiance has an updated look with a strong feeling of motion—one which clearly defines departments, creates a strong licensed goods department, and differentiates different shoe categories. Each area has similar fixtures, wall displays, and perforated metal canopies to highlight categories that are distinguished by variations in the color of the dyed wood and the painted metal. The materials employed reflect the collision between urban and natural environments: Man meets nature in the finishes and fixtures.

The curved aisle leading through the store serves as an "adventure trail," leading to a giant wall of video monitors. Echoing the curvaceous aisle is a ceiling that undulates, sweeps, and tapers from the entrance to the rear of the space. Constructed of two layers of gypsum board on individually cut and fitted studs, the ceiling is endowed with recessed downlights. Metal rods suspended from the ceiling support the narrow tail. Specialty lighting enhances the contrast between urban and natural moods: energy-efficient, high-intensity discharge lamps add "daylight" to the outdoor/hiking shoe area, while high-tech, low-voltage lamps allow "civilization" to intrude in the rear. Most of the lamps have been color-corrected to evoke a warm, outdoor feeling. The entire store is suggestive of an active lifestyle; signage, graphics, and banners all support the informal mood.

North Riverside, **Illinois**

Design: **Jon Greenberg & Associates**
Senior Project Executive: **Bob Berlin**
Senior Designer: **Gretchen Heinle**
Interior Designer: **Michele Martines**
Photography: **Laszlo Regos Photography**

"... the sporting

life begins with

the proper sports

shoes."

Orvis

For nearly 150 years, Orvis has been a sporting tradition in the United States; it has been the place to go for fishing and hunting equipment and clothing. This new 3,085-square-foot store, where customers will find sporting equipment, rugged outerwear, and even accessories for the home, is a cross between an old-fashioned country store and a stylish hunting lodge, all aglow with warm woods, stones, and other natural materials. The perimeter walls, dividers, and shelves are clear pine, and the floor is laid with random planks of heart pine. The fifteen-foot-high ceiling is patterned into a grid by criss-crossing beams of cherry and pine. Cherry wood is also used on some of the floor fixtures, many of which are trimmed with hickory bark. For visual relief, the rear wall is papered in a ticking pattern of hunter green.

In keeping with the atmospheric theme, the cash/wrap desk suggests the reception stand in a sports lodge; antlered chandeliers reinforce this imagery, while rustic furniture, made of wicker and "logs," help furnish the lodge. The designers also added other provincial accents like baskets, fieldstone, birch trees, and green foliage. There is even a waterfall rushing behind a hickory fence. To illuminate the space, track lights run the length of the ceiling along the long beams and spots are recessed into some of the squares formed by the timber grid.

Skokie, **Illinois**

Store Planning and Design: Norwood Oliver Design Associates, Inc.
Photography: Courtesy of The Orvis Company

Kinetix

In designing this prototype store for Kinetix, a company that promotes fitness, wellness, and community involvement, the designer's objective was to create "an inspiring, experimental atmosphere to appeal to a diverse array of active lifestyles." The 30,000-square-foot space consists of mostly "raw" materials—galvanized and distressed metals, waferboard, rubber and concrete flooring, inner tubes, bungee cords—conveying a youthful attitude of guts, integrity, and fundamentals. Fully detailed lifestyle areas are highlighted with information zones, and to sustain the high level of activity, visual displays feature fallen timber, a bubble tank, and a boat hung precariously off a wall. Large, hand-painted murals delineate departments and create lifestyle focal zones.

The circular floor plan positions the lifestyle shops around the perimeter. There is a central, raised platform for special events, a "deconstructivist" soft drink bar, and an interactive fitness zone with a bank of video monitors as its focal point. The wrap-around stockroom promotes high-quality service and efficiency. The creative visual merchandising and cross-selling techniques leave shoppers with the desire to return often.

Canton, **Ohio**

Design: Chute Gerdeman
Vice President, Design Director: Brian Shafley
Architect: Acciari Draeger Architects
Graphic Designer: Nottingham Spirk
Wall Murals: Kobalt Studios

For Kinetix
President: Jeff David

Photography: Rick Zaidan

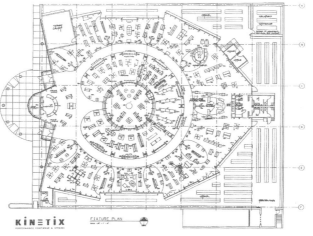

KINETIX
PERFORMANCE FOOTWEAR & APPAREL

FIXTURE PLAN

"... the designer's objective was to create an 'inspiring, experimental atmosphere to appeal to a diverse array of active lifestyles.' "

Sporting Eyes

Sporting Eyes is an example of just how focused lifestyle retailing has become. The fourteenth store in the parent company Iacon's group of specialty sunglasses shops, it is filled with popular lines of premier eyeglasses and sunglasses, as well as binoculars, swim goggles, and watches—all presented in 800 square feet of space. In response to the growing public interest in health and fitness, this rather focused concept was introduced by Iacon, who found that eyewear is most effectively merchandised when categorized by sport—even if the customer is a spectator rather than an athlete.

The wide though shallow space is warm and inviting. The sweeping arc of the cash/wrap counter fills most of the left-hand side of the store and is capped with a dropped fascia. On the right, vertical signage and graphics are complemented by display cabinets made of maple wood stained a luscious cantaloupe color. Conveying the lifestyle attitude of the shop are the arresting life-size action figures, sculpted in gesso, that are suspended from the high, black ceiling. The mountain biker, skier, fly fisherman, and snowboarder, for example, model the latest eyewear products in mini-boutique displays. A large-scale photomural of an Alpine snow scene on the rear wall serves as the backdrop for the skier and the snowboarder, while the fisherman dangles his feet from a timber pier floating overhead. The sports figures, the product display, and the retail space come alive in the focused lighting of intense halogen lamps that endow everything in the store with a high-style, high-energy feeling.

San Antonio, Texas

Design: Habitat Inc.
Photography: Rick Schreiber

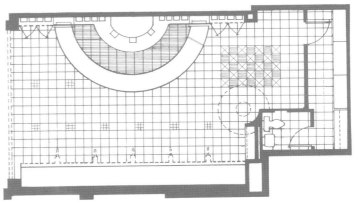

Fila

Fila is a highly recognizable name in sports apparel, and most sophisticated and educated active lifestyle enthusiasts recognize the brand name. Imagine their extra thrill in finding an outlet store where high quality Fila merchandise is available for less than the "boutique" price. To create an atmosphere that appeals to shoppers who are both knowledgeable and economical, designer Kambriz Fard took his inspiration from an urban playground. His design seemed to focus organically around chain-link material. "It's a great material," he explains. "You can attach things to it. It's strong but also airy, and most people immediately think of a playground when they see it."

Chain-link gates on wheels are positioned around the store's perimeter and merchandise is suspended from the links. Behind the gates, overstock is neatly contained in boxes. Most of the floor is plain concrete coated with a clear sealer. To enhance the playground concept and add color and excitement, children who win the Fila sponsored coloring contests are invited to reproduce their artwork on the concrete floors. The dark, open-deck ceiling and the metal shaded drop lights with halide lamps also contribute to a school gymnasium effect. Adding to the ambiance are natural wood fixtures, stainless steel trim, and exposed heating, ventilation, and air-conditioning systems.

Kenosha, Wisconsin

Design: **Imaginari**
Principal-in-charge: **Kambriz Fard**
Photography: Stephen Churchill Downes

Planet Reebok

By aiming to extend its appeal to a broader group of consumers, Reebok not only appeals to athletes, but to those who are interested in being fit for life. And if fitness is a motivating force in one's lifestyle, then the new Planet Reebok not only provides the inspiration, but presents the necessary footwear and apparel in a lively, interactive environment. By activating a touch sensor and monitor, potential shoppers in the street are linked to computerized screens in the display window, allowing interaction with the store, its message, and its merchandise—even when the store is closed. The interior of this 4,500-square-foot space is bold and uncomplicated, utilizing warm natural materials accented with metallic trim. Men's wear and women's wear are displayed separately, and custom-designed merchandising fixtures introduce and feature the most innovative footwear in each category. A video loop, at the bottom of each fixture, describes the attributes and benefits of each highlighted style. For shoppers' convenience, the appropriate footwear stock is housed adjacent to each sports category so that requested sizes and styles can be retrieved quickly and efficiently.

Sport-specific, mini-video monitors in the floor and the interactive kiosk in the center of the space contribute to the vitality of the design, while a "sports concierge" is available to answer questions about Reebok's history and product lines, as well as locations of sporting events in the New York metropolitan area. Endorsements by star athletes, sports memorabilia, and exciting graphics create strong visual elements for the store's merchandise and reinforce Reebok's identity by the incorporating the company's signature colors: white and reflex blue. All fixtures, graphics, and visuals are modular and mobile, and can be easily reconfigured to suit consumer needs.

New York, **New York**

Design: Fitch Inc.
Architect: Barry Koretz & Associates
Graphics: Fitch Inc. and C.I.T.E. Design
Interactive Window Display: Planet Interactive
Photography: Mark Steele, Fitch Inc.

"...Reebok not

only appeals to

athletes, but to

those who are

interested in being

fit for life."

Sneaker Stadium

Filled with seven vendor shops, plus "miles" of sports shoes organized by activity, this 15,000-square-foot space has a floor plan that is designed to resemble a running track. It not only sets the traffic pattern but also sets off the sports stadium image. Beneath the high deck ceiling, designers installed baseball and basketball scoreboards, pennants, banners, video monitors, and electronic reader boards to accentuate the sports arena feeling. The freestanding fixtures and vendor shops furnished with sports shoes and apparel occupy the center of the oval, while a giant wall of shoes lines the perimeter of the space.

Strong colors were selected to balance the bright colors typical of the vendors' merchandise, and the mobile purple valance that circles the perimeter wall maintains Sneaker Stadium's retail identity in the midst of competing vendor and brand name displays. Strong departmental and vendor signage also make it possible for sports enthusiasts to navigate the space easily and find the brand name, style, or type of shoe desired. A popular attraction at Sneaker Stadium is the half basketball court where anybody can shoot baskets or pick up a game. It fills up quickly in the afternoon after school gets out and the noise and activity lend real live excitement to the space. As part of the store's community involvement initiative, profits from coin-operated, sports-related games are donated to area school programs.

Springfield, **New Jersey**

Design: **Retail Planning Associates**
Sr. Vice President: Peter McIlroy
Vice President Project Director: Jeff McCall
Vice President, Director of Design Resources: Diane Rambo
Senior Designer: Paul Hamilton
Visual Communications Manager: Charles Mindigo
Senior Lighting Engineer: Perry Kotick
Photography: Charles Mindigo

Keds

Keds has long had a reputation as a "comfortable, affordable shoe," and was world famous well before Reebok or Nike. This 1,200-square-foot store in Miami, which represents the new prototype design, was created to update the Keds image, reflect the company's focus on style, and showcase several new lines of footwear for fashion-conscious consumers.

The space features three separate bays with six display panels dividing the area. Product lines are presented in lifestyle groupings where Plexiglas backdrops are silk-screened with graphics from Keds' packaging and abstractions of their current logos. While the color scheme of muted reds, blues, and white alludes to Ked's image as an all-American classic, the design firm of Pompei A.D. managed to create a contemporary, homey setting. Birch wall panels and slightly skewed display fixtures define an off-beat yet refined brand image. The asymmetrical pattern of the sisal-like floor covering is reflected in the ceiling grid. Adding to the domestic sensibility are ottomans, tables of assorted sizes, shapes, and textures, and the changeable graphic panels depicting active lifestyle activities and photos of local scenery. Videos are played on the sculpturesque bank of screens above the cash/wrap desk, adding movement, energy, and projecting the brand image without nostalgia.

Miami, **Florida**

Design: **Pompei A.D.**
Principal-in-charge: **Ron Pompei**
Project Manager: **Catherine Carr**

For Stride Rite
Director, Store Design and Construction: **Tracy Zaslow**
Senior Store Designer: **Cheryl Jablonski**
Construction Manager: **James Harte**

Photography: **John Gillan**

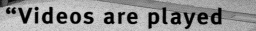

"Videos are played

on the

sculpturesque bank

of screens ...

adding movement,

energy, and projecting

the brand image

without nostalgia."

Hall of Fame Sports Store

Sports enthusiasts and memorabilia collectors will travel miles and miles for a card, a program, a ball—anything autographed by a sports great. Located in the popular, heavily touristed Faneuil Hall Festival Marketplace, the Hall of Fame Sports Store—part store, part museum—features sports collectibles, historic photography, and memorabilia.

The long, narrow floor plan of the 1,500-square-foot space is organized around a subtly curving, central display wall which originates at the rear of the store by a giant photo of Ted Williams—a great Boston baseball player. The arc in the soffit above travels towards the front of the store, mimicking the trajectory of a Williams home run hit. A series of display cases hang asymmetrically on the central wall. Each case represents a particular sport and incorporates authentic autographed photos, balls, programs, equipment—even uniforms. The oak floor is stained a deep green, the color of a baseball field, and the fixtures are constructed of cherry, maple, galvanized metal, and glass with brass hardware. Projecting over the counter and the display groupings are maple soffits. A final destination point, at the rear of the store, is a crescent-shaped area for viewing photos and videos.

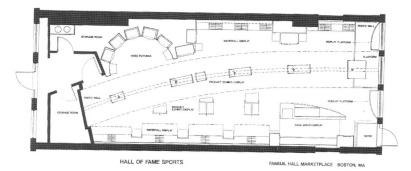

HALL OF FAME SPORTS   FANEUIL HALL MARKETPLACE BOSTON, MA

Design: Bergmeyer Associates, Inc.

Architect and Project Design Team: Robert M. Wood, Architects

Designer: Bill Neburka, Robert M. Wood

Project Manager: Peter Johnson

Graphics: Victoria Blaine Design

Photography: Lucy Chen Photography

Boston, **Massachusetts**

The North Face

For the sportsperson living in or near Chicago, a brand new lifestyle shopping option is now available in this flagship store for The North Face, a major manufacturer of outerwear, backpacks, sleeping bags, tents, ski apparel, and technical sportswear. Designed to offer a unique shopping environment where product merchandising and graphic display bring the outdoors experience to life, the 15,000-square-foot space is divided into six specific shopping zones on two levels.

The first level contains Performance Clothing. There, the Tekware Collection of clothes for trekking, climbing, and training offers shoppers versatility with outdoor apparel that doubles as weekend casual wear. Weather System, a second zone, houses outerwear for all weather conditions. A unique central stairway leads to the upper level, where the other four zones are located: Technical Skiwear (for Alpine skiers and snowboarders); Expedition Systems (layering garments for mountaineers, ice climbers, and cold-weather sports enthusiasts); Technical Footwear (shoes and boots); and the Equipment Zone. Here, on a climbing wall ten feet high and fourteen feet wide, shoppers can test shoes, boots, climbing gear, and apparel. In an open area just beyond the wall, customers are invited to set up tents on a variety of ground surfaces or try out sleeping bags for size and comfort.

Chicago, Illinois

Design: 555 Design Fabrication Management, Inc., Chicago
Principal-in-charge: James Geier
Vice President: Rick Marohn, AIA
Senior Designer: Peter Williamson
Architect: Gensler & Associates

For The North Face
Director of Retail: Thomas Goehring
Director of Visual Merchandising: Terrance R. Young
Graphic Design: Brett Critchlow

Photography: Peter Williamson, 555 DFM

That's Entertainment

With a plethora of entertainment and **amusement** options to choose from, it's no wonder that many people find the pursuit of entertainment a way of life. For some, it is a ***driving force***, a

strong need to be enveloped in a cocoon of bright lights, pulsating **music**, flashing images, and virtual **reality trips**. It is a life of music, television, films, excursions to Disney and Six Flags, and even the **contemplation of outer space**.

Music stores don't just sell records anymore. They are sources of entertainment: CDs, tapes, music videos, and ***laser discs***. They also sell the instruments of entertainment: televisions, compact disc **players**, total sound systems, computers and software, and now, complete home theater centers that bring all of the world of entertainment **into the home**. Wireless communications have also

become part of this network, providing people at home with **games** to play—alone or with someone else—or with ways to reach out to others on-line.

It is not surprising that stores that sell entertainment are themselves sources of entertainment. They are filled with color, **light**, **sound**, and *interactive* elements that invite shoppers to listen to Top Ten selections, preview videos, try computer games, or discover the intricacy and potential of wireless communications. Learning is made fun—and fun is what's for sale.

Cybersmith

For on-line lifestylers, Cybersmith is a new concept store filled with the latest computer technology. In an area of 4,000 square feet, the store features 33 computer stations, each of which can simultaneously accommodate three people. Here, customers can experiment with the Internet, on-line services, CD-ROMs, and computer games. They can even compose their own Web page or create a video greeting card.

Featuring a large, open facade with a view of the entire space, the overall feeling is dynamic yet friendly and comfortable—warm and welcoming yet contemporary in design. Much of the store is neutral gray accented with bright splashes of primary blue, red, and yellow. The natural wood floor fixtures and computer stations add to the warm ambiance. Dramatic overhead spots serve to highlight the wall displays and provide a stimulating, fun attitude. According to Jeff Pacione, vice president of the design firm Fitch, "The store was designed to accommodate both the computer-literate and the novice consumer, and I think the atmosphere will soften even the most technophobic customer."

Shopping at Cybersmith is definitely a hands-on experience. In addition to the computer stations there are also state-of-the-art "virtual reality pods" and "simulation stations" designed to keep customers busy and entertained—from the very young to the more mature. For a moment of relaxation and to prevent an early departure, there is the On-Line Cafe, where shoppers can order drinks, snacks, and light meals from computer stations.

Design: Fitch
Creative Directors: Jeff Pacione and Pamela Meade
Designers: Pamela Meade, Gideon Ansell, Ed Chung, Betty Lin, Jean-Andre Villamizar
Architect: Schwartz/Silver
Photographer: Mark Steele

White Plains, New York

Coconuts

Located only steps away from New York's famous Radio City Music Hall and Rockefeller Center, Coconuts had to make its presence known and its image felt. Architectural/design firm Jon Greenberg & Associates (JGA) joined forces with the graphic design firm Communication Arts to create a fresh look for the 18,000-square-foot, two-level space that was previously inhabited by another noted music chain. Three-dimensional signage takes the form of floating, gilded cherubs suspended above different departments.

On the main, street level of the store, for instance, cherubs donning baseball caps and sneakers hover above the rap section, while putti playing guitars fly over the rock and roll compact discs and tapes. Also located on this level are reggae, heavy metal, top ten, and music videos. On the second level, which is below street level, customers are greeted by a cherub with a violin, a computerized grand piano that plays concertos, and performances of operatic arias on laser disc. This more intimate level includes classical music, show tunes, country and western, and children's music.

The store is a music fan's dream. Walls of video monitors on both levels add music, movement, and excitement. Shoppers are invited to casually meander the floors, where the musical categories are clearly defined yet also blend into one another. JGA was responsible for the general layout and placement of departments and fixtures, the circulation patterns, and the cash/wrap stations. Communication Arts not only developed the signage and graphics, but was also responsible for infusing the store with elements of color and festivity.

New York, **New York**

Design: **Jon Greenberg & Associates**
Graphic Design: **Communication Arts**
Photography: **Laszlo Regos Photography**

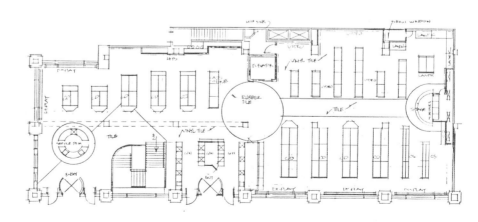

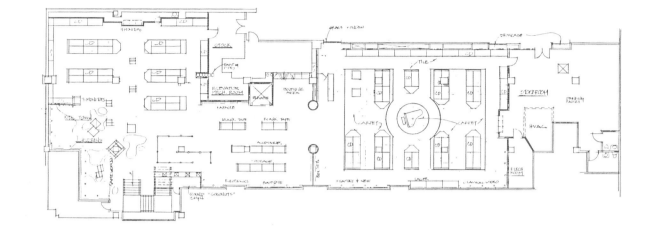

"The space

is a

music fan's

dream."

Strawberries

To introduce its new look, the music store Strawberries located its flagship store in a four-level, 12,000-square-foot space on Boylston Street, in Boston's trendy Back Bay area. Bergmeyer Associates developed a friendly, interactive interior design that both deftly communicates Strawberries' contemporary image and fits in with the existing urban fabric of the landmark exterior.

Upon entering the store, customers are immediately made aware of all four floors of merchandising. The elevator shaft is completely exposed to the third floor and a monumental, three-story stairway runs along one entire side of the space. Video monitors are suspended above the aisles and a whole wall at the rear of the main level, composed of twenty-seven video screens, is clearly visible from the street. Customers are invited to listen to selections of their choice from various categories of music at "Express" listening stations, many of which are equipped with coiling power cords and casters for mobility. Some of these stations are showcased in the facade windows, creating a "living display" where one might normally expect to see presentations of tapes, compact discs, and posters. Immovable listening stations are also located on the second and third floors, where they are fitted with benches for customers who prefer to sit down while they listen. As Strawberries is designed for music lovers of all ages, there is a themed area on the second floor catering especially to children, as well as a play area.

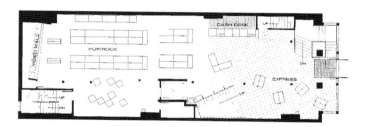

Boston, **Massachusetts**

Architect/Designer: Bergmeyer Associates, Inc.
Principal-in-charge: Ilkka T. Suvanto, RA
Project Manager: Juliette Bowker
Project Architect/Designer: Doug Coots
Photography: Lucy Chen Photography

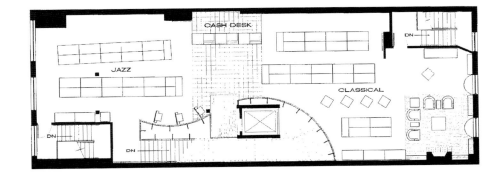

Music World

Montreal is world famous for the international jazz festival it hosts every summer, so it is no wonder that there is a tremendous market for recorded music and videos in this chic city. With its 6,000-square-foot store in the Complexe Desjardins, this Music World location, which boasts something for everyone's musical pleasure, is the largest in the growing Canadian chain. The industrial warehouse space is divided into easily recognizable specialty sections, where architectural detailing and color palette figuratively represent the types of music found in each area.

Metal structural elements, wood beams, and hanging lighting fixtures, for example, conjure up images of a "Rock Garage" for the store's rock and roll, rap, and alternative music departments. For jazz enthusiasts, pictorial elements from the work of Joan Miró and other artists who lived in Paris in the 1920s define this section. Hovering above a cornice, a painted blue sky sets the stage for the classical music department. The Sputnik lamp, representing the overall spirit of the store, hangs in the center of the "sky" of this more subdued department, tying it in with the rest.

The store is distinguished by its industrial cash counters and a giant video projection screen. But dominating the space is the Listening Bar, located on a platform at the front of the store, alongside the facade windows. Clearly visible from the street, the bar contributes a great deal of animation to the space. Overall, Music World reflects an eclecticism and a tribalism evocative of the "world beat" sensibility found in today's music and in contemporary culture at large.

Montreal, Canada

Design: Gervais Harding and Associates Design Inc.
Principal-in-charge: Steve Sutton
Senior Designer: Sophie Lemarbre
Senior Technician: Pierre Emard
Technician: Carlo Peruch
Photography: Yves Lefebvre

...a tribalism evocative of the

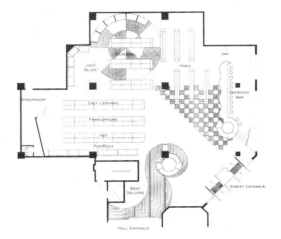

world beat'...in today's music..."

Salem Power Station

The young and progressive market in this rapidly developing country has honed in on the "world beat" of the music, fashion, and American lifestyle that is fast unifying young people worldwide. A satellite operation of Salem cigarettes, this music store, located in the Lot 10 Shopping Center in Kuala Lumpur, is linked with Salem's advertising and promotional strategies.

The materials—all high-tech, glistening and industrial—reflect the energy and youth of the core group of customers. The neutral "power station" is made up of a potent combination of aluminum, stainless steel, perforated and embossed metals, and glass. Different categories of music are identified by aluminum, checkered plate floors, which serve as circulation zones. Surrounding a structural column up front are two tiers of video monitors that create movement, while below, colorful graphics and boat-shaped shelves display new releases and featured performers. White terrazzo floors further set off this area. In keeping with the progressive character of the store, all compact disc and cassette tape gondolas are movable and adaptable to changing merchandise requirements. A long service counter is faced with natural wood and highlighted with stainless steel fins.

Curving metal walls, stairways with pipe railings, exposed ductwork, and metal-sheathed columns all contribute to the look and feel of the "power station" A platform at the rear of the space serves as a retreat for a relaxed cup of coffee and also doubles as a performance stage for visiting musical groups.

Kuala Lumpur, **Malaysia**

Design: Axis Network
Principal-in-charge: Foo Fatt Chuen
Photography: David Lau

153

Gerngross

As part of the total renovation of the Gerngross department store in Vienna, the company hired the design firm and fitting manufacturer Umdasch to redesign and expand its entertainment area. In contrast to most music stores, which cater almost exclusively to young people, this department is aimed at a more mature market.

The space itself is neutral in color and contemporary in concept. Umdasch created and installed modular walls and floor fittings to create a flexible, customer friendly retail space. The floor fixtures are composed of black lacquered metal frames with off-white plastic laminate panels and shelving. High tech metallic textures were added to make the department appear more up-to-date without being too active. The wall system consists of black uprights clad with wire grids, and perforated metal, slotted, or laminated panels, depending on the product to be displayed. All fixtures have flexibility built into them and are fully adjustable.

A gray terrazzo aisle divides the rest of the space, which is covered with gray-green carpeting. The walls and ceiling are painted off-white. In addition to the square fluorescent fixtures embedded in the acoustical tile ceiling, wire frames carry the track lights that are used to highlight feature displays on the floor and walls. A row of video monitors are suspended over the central display area of the department, adding drama and excitement to an otherwise subdued area.

Vienna, **Austria**

Design: Umdasch Store Planning
Planning and Design: Erwin Gugerell
Fittings: Umdasch Shop Concept
Photography: Umdasch Shop-Concept GMBH

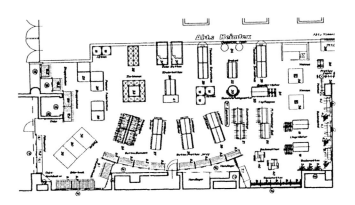

Sony Style

Whether it is for the home or the office, for business or for pleasure, there is always room for a Sony in your life. To create a consumer-friendly shopping experience wherein customers can comfortably interact with Sony electronics, music, and movies, the company commissioned New York-based designer James Mansour Ltd. to provide a stimulating and sophisticated background for their products. A warm, monochromatic color scheme and streamlined, innovative fixtures effectively convey the company style. Each fixture is a unique and technical masterpiece providing maximum flexibility for various electronic and interactive appliances, while creating a sleek, inviting impression.

On the lower level, Mansour created a replica of a 1930s Hollywood lounge where shoppers can relax and appreciate the myriad aspects of Sony home entertainment systems. Intimate groupings of Art Deco-style furnishings are equipped with television sets and speakers, while audio components on elegant, trolley-like wood units are wheeled past the seated customers. The beauty of this system, explains Mansour, is that "you can test the equipment as if you were at home, relaxing on a stylish, ergonomically correct couch, sipping cappuccino, and nibbling delicious pastries."

Finally, to prove that high technology can also be stylish, fashion designer Donna Karan wardrobed the lounge staff with unisex pantsuits. The screening room, which is a state-of-the-art audio theater, was decorated by Ralph Lauren. Interior design, fashion, entertainment, electronics, music, and romance create a seamless experience at Sony Style, providing ample opportunity to savor a lifestyle you may have only read about.

New York, **New York**

Design: James Mansour Ltd.
Project Team: James Mansour, William Koo, Manon Zinzell
Photography: Antoine Bootz

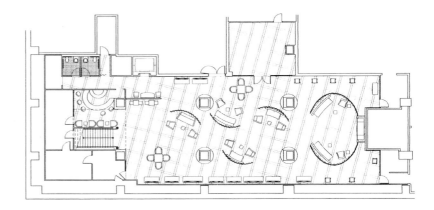

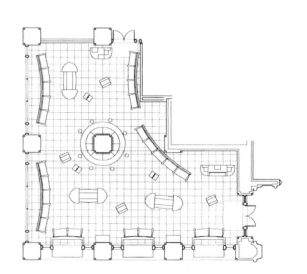

SONY PLAZA
RETAIL SOUTH

Leader Communications

As more people begin to work from their homes, good communication with the world outside not only takes on a heightened significance, but is a daily necessity. The home office is fast becoming the prime site of a new lifestyle, in which high technology plays a major role. Leader Communications, a 5,000-square-foot exhibition and retail center, was designed to showcase emerging wireless technologies for Cellular One.

The design plan resembles an open market with a front desk made of stone. Curved banners form canopies over the manufacturer's products, which are displayed on easels below. Floor patterns and an explosive graphic with the message "Get Activated" lead shoppers past the accessories counter ("The Right Stuff") to a service area on the floor below, where a large, circular arena dominates. Equipped with seats and a rolling projection screen, the arena is the spot for large-scale special events and demonstrations. In the midst of this technological playground, "Get Wired" is a literal invitation for adults to take an espresso break before continuing on to sample more of the high-tech attractions.

The interactive exhibit that receives the most attention from visitors is called "The Wheel of Misfortune," a game which allows customers to solve problems and reduce stress by means of Motorola-produced wireless technology. The Advance Life Cycle testing exhibit, also Motorola sponsored, tests the durability of telephone units. To create this dynamic setting, the designers specified a potent mixture of materials, ranging from concrete, stone, slate, and terrazzo, to clear and stained maple, to carpeting and acrylics.

Design: Stephen Wierzbowski, WDW Design, with
Paul Florian, Florian Architecture
Project Architects: Sergio Guardia, Florian Architecture,
Robert Lynn, WDW Design
Graphic Design: Lora Wierzbowski, WDW Design
Photography: John Frangoulis

Chicago, **Illinois**

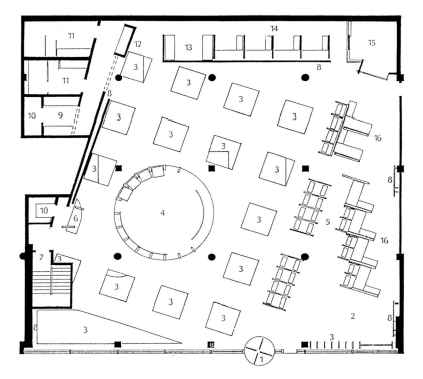

ON AIR
Time Warner Wireless

The same company that has entertained millions of families with Bugs Bunny and Batman is now incorporating entertainment and fun into its wireless retail operation. Introducing a brand new direction in retailing telecommunications, cable, and information services, the 3,000-square-foot Time Warner store is a marketing and technology showcase for the company's wireless communications systems. Designed for customers with busy lifestyles and who spend a good deal of time on-line, the store features user-friendly, hands-on, one-stop shopping for cellular, paging, and cable services.

The primary challenge for the designers was to create a retail environment that conveys the sense of freedom achieved through the use of wireless communications. To accomplish this, the store is divided into five departments: Cellular, Cable, Paging, Accessories, and What's New—an area focusing on lifestyle trends, new products, and state-of-the-art, interactive software programs.

The mostly neutrally packaged products are presented in a space that is dramatically lit and accented with the company's signature colors: bright yellow and vibrant blue. The interactive floor and wall fixtures are finished with blue and yellow laminates, while images of classic film stars like Ingrid Bergman and Ray Milland share the space with the colorful graphics. Technical information and product layout are crisply organized and color-coded. Yellow grids float from the dark blue ceiling, echoing the undulating white aisle that leads shoppers to the rear of the store. Here, in a wood-paneled area, cable products are presented on an oversize video screen, while throughout the store, Time Warner videos are continuously played on television monitors.

162

Design: **West 49 Parallel Design**
Audio Visual: **Bergmeyer Associates, Inc.**
Contractor: **Richter & Ratner**
Graphics: **Time Inc. Promotion Group**
Art Director: **Paul Kuhn**
Photography: **David Lamb Photography**

Rochester, **New York**

Kay Bee Toys

For children, being let loose in a free-to-touch toy store is the ultimate shopping experience, and when the shopping is easy, it can be enjoyable for parents as well. With a design that possesses wit, verve, and personality, this new Kay Bee store is filled with energy. It has neither an industrial warehouse feeling, where floor-to-ceiling shelves are often stacked with unreachable toys, nor a precious, suffocating cuteness that other children's stores affect.

Natural wood floors and clean white laminate and metal wall and floor fixtures create an impression of openness in the long, narrow space. Turquoise banners with yellow letters, directing customers to specific categories of merchandise, float overhead from the well illuminated, white ceiling. The massive duct system is also painted turquoise, accenting the fixtures. While not competing with the product display, neon ribbons running the length of the store add sizzle and panache.

Merchandise is stacked on wall units to heights that are conveniently within reach. The white laminate cash/wrap counters in the center of the space are highlighted by signage and white metal drop lights. The facade is distinguished by a sweeping turquoise fascia that bows out over the entrance and is decorated with the same neon ribbons employed inside the store, as well as the store's logo, which is repeated on the entry floor.

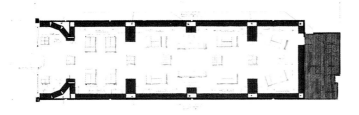

Design: Fitzpatrick Design Group, Inc.
President and Creative Director: Jay Fitzpatrick
Project Manager: Michael Dubiel
Project Designer: Andrew McQuilkin
Director of Color and Materials: Lisa Benson
Architect: Rudy Rodriguez, Norman DiChiara Architects, PC

For Melville (Parent Company)
Director of Store Planning: Richard Brunetti
Architectural Project Manager: Rich Stuerzel

For Kay Bee Toy Stores
Vice President, Visual Presentation/Store Design: Nick Seufert
Vice President, Real Estate Construction : Tony Palino

Photography: Fred Charles

Massapequa, **New York**

GAMES

VIDEO

PRESCHOOL

SPORTS

"...Being let loose in a free-to-touch toy store is the ultimate shopping experience..."

Another Universe

For people who enjoy escaping into outer space, and for those to whom science fiction is more real than real life, Another Universe is a virtual paradise. In this new prototype store, the science fiction aficionado will find books, games, graphics, and other related materials. The design synthesizes forms and materials into a vocabulary that complements the merchandise and store theme, without overtly borrowing or relying too heavily on typical science fiction imagery.

As the space is small and the merchandise varied, three significant design elements maintain a sense of order and direction: the sales desk, the curved display wall equipped with video monitors, and the circular comics area. Each is intended to read as an individual—though related—area. The cash/wrap counter is constructed of laminated sheet metal reinforced with "floating," hexagonal ceiling panels. A translucent Plexiglass ceiling covers the comics area while the remainder of the ceiling is left exposed to accommodate the flexible merchandise lighting. The slate tiles on the entry floor contrast with the carpet patterns throughout the rest of the store.

Most of the walls are paneled with matte, metallic-gray slatwall accented with shiny lines. Matching floor gondolas are also gray, with the slatwall employed as end caps. Dynamic, floor-to-ceiling fins painted school-bus yellow divide the monitor wall into specialized segments for stocking videos and other related products. Highlighting the "out of this world" shopping experience is an "alien" in a hexagonal glass enclosure surrounded by a stainless-steel skeletal representation of a space ship.

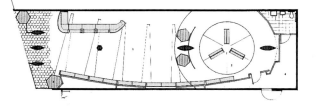

Fairfax, **Virginia**

Designer/Architect: **Core**
Peter F. Hapstak III, AIA , IIDA
Dale A. Stewart, AIA, Anthony Maher, AIA
Lighting Consultant: Coventry Lighting
Photography: Apertures, Inc., Thomas Humphrey

Directory

Stores

Another Universe
11750 Fair Oaks Drive
Fairfax, Virginia 22123
Tel: (703) 361-9000

The Bottler's Shop
Avenida Kennedy 9001 #3050
Alto Las Condes Mall
Santiago
Chile
Tel: 562 2131 233

**British Columbia
& Beyond**
c/o Host Marriott - P.O. Box 23630
Main Terminal, 4th Floor,
Room 4187
Airport Postal Outlet
Richmond, British Columbia
V7B 1X1
Canada
Tel: (604) 231-3731
Fax: (604) 231-3732

Children in Paradise
909 North Rush Street
Chicago, Illinois 60611
Tel: (312) 951-KIDS

Coconuts Music and Video
405 Sixth Avenue
New York, New York 10014
Tel: (212) 243-1446

Cybersmith
125 Westchester Avenue
White Plains, New York 10601
Tel: (914) 686-3570

**Detroit Institute of Arts
Museum Shop**
27500 Novi Road
Novi, Michigan 48377
Tel: (810) 380-8050

Dillons
128 New Street
Birmingham B2 4DB
England
Tel: 44-121-631-4333

Discovery Channel Store
2326 The Strand
Galveston, Texas 77550
Tel: (409) 735-5755

Domain
290 Route 4 East
Paramus, New Jersey 07652
Tel: (201) 487-4222

Eddie Bauer
250 Post Street
San Francisco, California 94108
Tel: (415) 986-7600

Fila
11211 120th Avenue
Kenosha, Wisconsin 53142
Tel: (414) 857-7887

The Finish Line
7501 Cermak Road
North Riverside, Illinois 60546
Tel: (708) 442-7552

Fitigues
939 North Rush Street
Chicago, Illinois
Tel: (312) 943-8676
Fax: (312) 943-3081

Gallerie Lassen
The Forum Shops
3500 South Las Vegas Boulevard
Suite D1
Las Vegas, Nevada 89109

**The Garden Shop of the
Chicago Botanic Garden**
1000 Lake Cook Road
Glencoe, Illinois 60022
Tel: (847) 835-8206

Gerngross Kaufhaus AG
Mariahilfer Strasse 38-48
A-1070 Vienna
Austria
Tel: 222/52 180-0
Fax: 222/52 180-239

Globe Corner Bookstore
500 Boylston Street
Boston, Massachusetts 02116
Tel: (617) 859-8008

Guess?
80 Newbury Street
Boston, Massachusetts 02116
Tel: (617) 236-4147
Fax: (627) 236-5183

Hall of Fame Sports Store
Faneuil Hall Marketplace
North Market Building, First Floor
Boston, Massachusetts 02109
Tel: (617) 227-1424

Hechinger
210 Fort Mead Road
Laurel, Maryland 20707
Tel: (301) 604-5061

**Herman's The Sports Store
of New York**
30 Rockefeller Plaza
New York, New York 10020
Tel: (212) 541-6630
Fax: (212) 541-9439

IKEA Marketing Outpost
131 East 57th Street
New York, New York 10022
Tel: (212) 308-IKEA

Kay Bee Toys
1137 Sunrise Mall, Space #3
Sunrise Highway & Carmen Road
Massapequa, New York 11758
Tel: (516) 541-7193

Keds
Dadeland Mall
7535 North Kendall Drive
Miami, Florida 33156
Tel: (305) 668-4755

Kinetix
4640 Whipple Road, NW
North Canton, Ohio 44735
Tel: (216) 490-2602
Fax: (216) 497-4499

Kitchen Bazaar
Hulen Mall
4800 South Hulen Street
Fort Worth, Texas 76132
Tel: (301) 210-5331
Fax: (301) 419-5236

Lacoste Boutique
9700 Collins Avenue
Bal Harbour, Florida 33154
Tel: (212) 418-0729

**Leader Communications/
Motorola Exhibits**
170 West Ontario
Chicago, Illinois 60610
Tel: (312) 692-7800
Fax: (312) 642-7683

Mega Mart
700 South 72nd Street
Omaha, Nebraska 68114
Tel: (402) 397-6100
Fax: (402) 392-3349

**Museum of Fine Arts,
Boston**
Mall at Chestnut Hill
199 Boylston Street
Chestnut Hill, Massachusetts 02167
Tel: (617) 964-8101

**Music World
Complexe Desjardins**
1, Complexe Desjardins
Montreal H5B 1B8
Canada
Tel: (416) 234-9211
Fax: (416) 234-9213

The North Face
875 North Michigan Avenue
Chicago, Illinois 60611
Tel: (312) 337-7200
Fax: (312) 867-2500

**Old Navy Clothing
Company**
610 Avenue of the Americas
New York, New York 10011
Tel: (212) 645-0663

ON AIR

Time Warner Wireless
205 Summit Pointe Drive, Suite 2
Rochester, New York 14467
Tel: (716) 321-1400

The Original Levi's Store
3 East 57th Street
New York, New York 10022
Tel: (212) 838-2188

Orvis
Space J1A
Old Orchard Shopping Center
Old Orchard Road &
Skokie Boulevard
Skokie, Illinois 60077
Tel: (708) 677-4774

Oshman's SuperSports U.S.A.
1101 SuperMall Way
Auburn, Washington 98001
Tel: (713) 967-8747
Fax: (713) 967-8288

Out of the West
1000 West Armitage
Chicago, Illinois 60614
Tel: (312) 404-9378
Fax: (312) 404-0797

Planet Reebok
Lincoln Square
160 Columbus Avenue
New York, New York 10023
Tel: (617) 341-5000

Pottery Barn
2100 Chestnut Street
San Francisco, California 94123
Tel: (415) 421-7900

**Robert Dyas
The Ironmongers**
Peterfield
Hampshire
England

Salem Power Station
Lot 10 Shopping Centre
Jalan Sultan Ismail
Kuala Lumpur
Malaysia
Tel: (603) 244-2890

Scott Shuptrine
977 East 14 Mile Road
Troy, Michigan 48083
Tel: (810) 589-1100
Fax: (810) 589-1146

Smith & Hawken
394 West Broadway
New York, New York 10012
Tel: (212) 925-1190
Fax: (212) 925-4894

Sneaker Stadium
345 Route 22 East
Springfield, New Jersey 07081
Tel: (908) 248-9090
Fax: (908) 248-9049

Sony Style
550 Madison Avenue
New York, New York 10022
Tel: (212) 833-8800
Fax: (212) 833-4181

Sporting Eyes
849 East Commerce Avenue, Space 239
San Antonio, Texas 78205
Tel: (602) 451-3958
Fax: (602) 451-3879

Strawberries
761 Boylston Street
Boston, Massachusetts 02116
Tel: (617) 262-8686

UCLA Spirit
Citywalk
1000 Universal Center Drive
Universal City, California 91608
Tel: (818) 754-6720

Voyagers, The Travel Store
19009 Preston Road, Suite 300
Dallas, Texas 75252
Tel: (214) 732-9373

WH Smith
1000 El Conquistador Avenue
El Conquistador Hotel Resort
Las Croabas
Fajardo, Puerto Rico 00738
Tel: (404) 618-2790
Fax: (404) 951-1352

William Ashley China
95 Bloor Street West
Toronto M4W3V1
Canada
Tel: (416) 964-9111
Fax: (416) 960-9348

Architecture & Design Firms

555 Design Fabrication Management, Inc.
1238 South Ashland Avenue
Chicago, Illinois 60608
Tel: (312) 733-6777
Fax: (312) 733-3083

Acciari Draegar Architects
17710 Detroit Avenue
Lakewood, Ohio 44107
Tel: (216) 521-5134
Fax: (216) 521-4824

AM Partners, Inc.
1164 Bishop Street, Suite 1000
Honolulu, Hawaii 96813
Tel: (808) 526-2828
Fax: (808) 538-0027

Associated Students UCLA
308 Westwood Plaza, KH 212A
Los Angeles, California 90024
Tel: (310) 825-6161
Fax: (310) 206-4563

Axis Network
Suite 7.15 7th Floor, Wisma Central
Jalan Ampang
Kuala Lumpur
Malaysia
Tel: (603) 263-4181
Fax: (603) 263-4186

Backen Arrigoni & Ross, Inc.
1660 Bush Street
San Francisco, California 94109
Tel: (415) 536-2266
Fax: (415) 536-2323

Barry Koretz & Associates
142 Crescent Street
Brockton, Massachusetts 02402
Tel: (508) 583-5603
Fax: (508) 536-2914

Bergmeyer Associates, Inc.
286 Congress Street
Boston, Massachusetts 02210
Tel: (617) 542-1025
Fax: (617) 338-6897

Brand + Allen Architects, Inc.
1400 Post Oak Boulevard, Suite 200
Houston, Texas 77056
Tel: (713) 621-7227
Fax: (713) 621-7393

Christopher Barriscale Architects
72 Spring Street
New York, New York 10012
Tel: (212) 274-1205
Fax: (212) 343-1544

Chute Gerdeman
130 East Chestnut Street
Columbus, Ohio 43215
Tel: (614) 469-1001
Fax: (614) 469-1002

Core
1010 Wisconsin Avenue NW
Washington, D.C. 20007
Tel: (202) 466-6116
Fax: (202) 466-6235

Crabtree Hall/Plan Creatif
70 Crabtree Lane
London SW6 6LT
England
Tel: 171 381 8755
Fax: 171 385 9575

Eva Maddox Associates, Inc.
300 West Hubbard Street, Suite 201
Chicago, Illinois 60610
Tel: (312) 670-0092
Fax: (312) 670-2624

Feola Carli Archuleta
116 East Broadway
Glendale, California 91205
Tel: (818) 247-9020
Fax: (818) 247-9413

Fitch
Commonwealth House
1 New Oxford Street
London WCIA IWW
England
Tel: 171 208 8000
Fax: 171 208 0200

Fitch Inc.
10350 Olentangy River Road
Worthington, Ohio 43085
Tel: (614) 885-3453
Fax: (614) 885-4289

Fitch Inc.
139 Lewis Wharf
Boston, Massachusetts 02110
Tel: (617) 367-1491
Fax: (617) 367-1996

Fitzpatrick Design Group
2109 Broadway, Suite 203
New York, New York 10023
Tel: (212) 580-5842
Fax: (212) 580-5849

Florian Architecture
432 North Clark, Suite 200
Chicago, Illinois 60610
Tel: (312) 670-0220
Fax: (312) 670-2221

FRCH Design Worldwide
860 Broadway
New York, New York 10003
Tel: (212) 254-1229
Fax: (212) 982-5543

GAP, Inc.
1 Harrison Street, 6th Floor
San Francisco, California 94105
Tel: (415) 291-2225
Fax: (415) 291-2629

Gervais Harding and
Associates Design Inc.
275 St. Jacques Ouest, First Floor
Montreal, Quebec H2Y IM9
Canada
Tel: (514) 843-5812
Fax: (514) 843-5984

Grid/3 International, Inc.
37 West 39 Street, 12th Floor
New York, New York 10018
Tel: (212) 391-1162
Fax: (212) 575-2391

Guess Inc.
1444 South Alameda Avenue
Los Angeles, California 90036
Tel: (213) 765-3132

Habitat, Inc.
6031 South Maple Avenue
Tempe, Arizona 85283
Tel: (602) 345-8442
Fax: (602) 730-0188

Hill/Glazier Architects,
Inc.
700 Welch Road
Palo Alto, California 94304
Tel: (415) 617-0366
Fax: (415) 617-0373

Iceberg
Irarrazaval 363
Santiago
Chile

Imaginari
1437 Seventh Street, Suite 340
Santa Monica, California 90401
Tel: (310) 393-9111
Fax: (310) 458-2843

James Mansour Ltd.
495 Broadway, Second Floor
New York, New York 10012
Tel: (212) 941-0970
Fax: (212) 941-6387

Jon Greenberg &
Associates, Inc.
29355 Northwestern Highway
Suite 300
Southfield, Michigan 48034
Tel: (810) 355-0890
Fax: (810) 351-3062

Marvin Herman &
Associates
1203 North State Parkway
Chicago, Illinois 60613
Tel: (312) 787-0347
Fax: (312) 787-0204

Michael Malone
Architects, Inc.
13355 Noel Road, Suite 1310, LB 58
Dallas, Texas 75240
Tel: (214) 702-7960
Fax: (214) 702-7975

Norman DiChiara
Architects, PC
15 Fisher Lane, Suite 201
White Plains, New York 10603
Tel: (914) 993-0500
Fax: (914) 993-0586

Norwood Oliver Design
Associates, Inc.
501 American Legion Way
Point Pleasant Beach, New Jersey
08742
Tel: (908) 295-1200
Fax: (908) 899-4680

Oshman's Sporting Goods
2303 Maxwell Lane
Houston, Texas 77023
Tel: (713) 967-8747
Fax: (713) 967-8295

Pompei A.D.
394 West Broadway, Second Floor
New York, New York 10012
Tel: (212) 431-1262
Fax: (212) 966-8659

Ralph Choeff Architect, PA
3909 NE 163rd Street, Suite 210
North Miami Beach, Florida 33160
Tel: (305) 940-7662
Fax: (305) 945-0019

The Retail Group
2025 1st Avenue, Suite 470
Seattle, Washington 98121
Tel: (206) 441-8330
Fax: (206) 441-8710

Retail Planning
Associates, L.P.
645 South Grant Avenue
Columbus, Ohio 43206
Tel: (614) 461-1820
Fax: (614) 461-7195

Schafer Associates, Inc.
635 Butterfield Road
Oakbrook Terrace, Illinois 60181
Tel: (708) 932-8787
Fax: (708) 932-8788

Schwartz/Silver
530 Atlantic Avenue
Boston, Massachusetts 02210
Tel: (617) 542-6650
Fax: (617) 951-0779

Sunderland Innerspace
Design Inc.
688 West Hastings Street, Suite 610
Vancouver, British Columbia
V6B 1P1
Canada
Tel: (604) 662-7015
Fax: (604) 662-7018

Harry Swihart, Architect
1535 North Dayton
Chicago, Illinois 60622
Tel: (312) 255-8866
Fax: (312) 255-8868

Umdasch Shop-Concept
GMBH
Reichsstrasse 23
A-3300 Amstetten
Austria
Tel: 7472/605-0
Fax: 7472/605-722

Walker Group/CNI
320 West 13th Street
New York, New York 10014
Tel: (212) 206-0444
Fax: (212) 645-0461

WDW Design
53 West Jackson Boulevard #1800N
Chicago, Illinois 60604
Tel: (312) 362-1200
Fax: (312) 362-1204

West 49 Parallel
Design Inc.
14 Clarence Square, Main Floor
Toronto, Ontario M5V1H1
Canada
Tel: (416) 593-6732
Fax: (416) 593-6791

Photographers

Dorothée Ahrens
130 West 25th Street
New York, New York 10001
Tel: (212) 741-9574
Fax: (212) 242-4401

Apertures, Inc.
Thomas Humphrey
11817 Blue Spruce Road
Reston, Virginia 22091
Tel: (703) 860-3866
Fax: (703) 860-3870

ASUCLA
308 Westwood Plaza, KH 212A
Los Angeles, California 90024
Tel: (310) 825-6161
Fax: (310) 206-4563

Paul Bielenberg
6823 Pacific View Drive
Los Angeles, California 90068
Tel: (213) 874-9951
Fax: (213) 874-1907

Tom Blewden
Fitch
Commonwealth House
1 New Oxford Street
London WCIA IWW
England
Tel: 171 208 8000
Fax: 171 208 0200

Antoine Bootz
123 West 20th Street
New York, New York 10011
Tel: (212) 366-9041
Fax: (212) 366-9386

Andrew Bordwin
70A Greenwich Avenue #332
New York, New York 10011
Tel: (212) 633-0383
Fax: (212) 633-1046

Bob Briskey
Briskey Photography
306 South Vine Street
Hinsdale, Illinois 60521
Tel: (708) 655-8965
Fax: (708) 655-8957

Marcella Castello
Los Arucanos 2302
Santiago
Chile
Tel: (562) 232-3316

Fred Charles
254 Park Avenue South
New York, New York 10010
Tel: (212) 505-0686
Fax: (212) 505-0692

Chris Leavitt Photography
2012 South 320th Street, Suite M
Federal Way, Washington 98003

Peter Cook
300 Saint Johns Street
London ECIV4PP
England

David Lamb Photography
10 Beardsley Street
Fairport, New York 14450
Tel: (716) 377-4080
Fax: (716) 377-0740

Stephen Churchill Downes
New York, New York
Tel: (212) 674-0790

Douglas Dun
Backen Arrigoni & Ross
1660 Bush Street
San Francisco, California 94109
Tel: (415) 536-2208
Fax: (415) 536-2323

John Frangoulis
114 West Illinois
Chicago, Illinois 60610
Tel: (312) 822-0617
Fax: (312) 822-0960

John Gillan
13101 SW 14th Place
Fort Lauderdale, Florida 33325
Tel: (954) 236-3556
Fax: (954) 236-3996

Steve Hall
Hedrich-Blessing
11 West Illinois
Chicago, Illinois 60610
Tel: (312) 321-1151

Craig Harold
2737 59th Avenue SW
Seattle, Washington 98116
Tel: (206) 933-6740
Fax: (206) 938-0389

HNK Architectural Photography, Inc.
610 Green Bay Road
Highland Park, Illinois 60035
Tel: (847) 433-6666

Chris Hollick
40 Montague Road
Southall
Middlesex UB2 5PD
England
Tel: 181 843 9493

Edi Ignacio
GAP Inc.
1 Harrison Street, 6th Floor
San Francisco, California 94105
Tel: (415) 291-2116
Fax: (415) 291-2629

Richard Johnson
Interior Images
100 Woodmount Avenue
Toronto, Ontario
Canada
Tel: (416) 467-4620
Fax: (416) 467-9894

Jud Haggard Photography
4620 Holt Street
Bellaire, Texas 77401
Tel: (713) 667-0092

Craig Kuhner
2006 Heatherway Drive
Arlington, Texas 76012
Tel: (817) 265-9676

Chun Y Lai
428 Broome Street
New York, New York 10013
Tel: (212) 966-5025
Fax: (212) 966-5090

Laszlo Regos Photography
Jon Greenberg & Associates
29355 Northwestern Highway
Southfield, Michigan 48034
Tel: (810) 355-0890
Fax: (810) 351-3062

David Lau
Hilton Photographers Kuala Lumpur
No. 15 Tengkat Tong Shin
50200 Kuala Lumpur
Malaysia
Tel: (603) 242-3420
Fax: (603) 241-2119

Yves Lefebvre
5223 Earnschliffe
Montreal, Quebec H3X2P7
Canada
Tel: (514) 486-4255

John Linden
220 Lavderdale Mansions
Laverdale Road
Maida Vale
London W9 INQ
Tel: 44 171 289 8525

Lucy Chen Photography
1 Fitchburg Street, C105
Somerville, Massachusetts 02143
Tel: (617) 625-1008
Fax: (617) 625-1220

Charles Mindigo
Retail Planning Associates
645 South Grant Avenue
Columbus, Ohio 43206
Tel: (614) 461-1820
Fax: (614) 461-7195

Rob Melnychuk Photography, Inc.
204 1807 Fir Street
Vancover, British Columbia V6J3a5
Canada
Tel: (604) 736-8066
Fax: (604) 736-9339

Rick Schreiber
Habitat, Inc.
6031 South Maple Avenue
Tempe, Arizona 85283
Tel: (602) 345-8442
Fax: (602) 730-0188

Mark Steele
Fitch Inc.
139 Lewis Wharf
Boston, Massachusetts 02110
Tel: (617) 367-1491
Fax: (617) 367-1996

Steinkamp Ballogg Photography
666 West Hubbard
Chicago, Illinois 60610
Tel: (312) 421-1233
Fax: (312) 421-1241

John Stillman
Photo Dimension
1112 Jefferson Street
Hollywood, Florida 33019
Tel: (954) 922-9887
Fax: (954) 922-9719

Umdasch Shop-Concept GMBH
Reichsstrasse 23
A-3300 Amstetten
Austria
Tel: 7472/605-0
Fax: 7472/605-722

Peter Williamson
555 DFM
1238 South Ashland Avenue
Chicago, Illinois 60608
Tel: (312) 733-6777
Fax: (312) 733-3083

Rick Zaidan
1668 State Road
Cuyahoga Falls, Ohio 44223
Tel: (216) 920-8142

Index

Stores

Architects & Designers

Photographers

Acknowledgments: My Thanks to the many architects, designers, store planners, visual merchandisers, and PR persons who have, over the years, made my professional life as a writer/editor a pleasure. With their help and their projects they have made each book an adventure and a voyage of discovery. May we keep sailing along together finding new and exciting ports of call in the retail field.